I Had a Twin

Disrupting the Cycle of Childhood Trauma

Pamela Byrd

I Had a Twin

Disrupting the Cycle of Childhood Trauma

Pamela Byrd

Independently Published

ISBN#: 978-0-578-39749-8

First Edition

Editor: Mary Marvella Edits

Cover Photos: Chatman Photography

Cover Design: Big Ben, Inc.

Printed in the United States of America

Dedication

I dedicate this book to my two sisters, Cheryl and Angie whose love surrounded me all the years of their lives. No matter how geographically distant we were on our journeys, we always shared the same room in our hearts.

Acknowledgments

I first give honor and praise to my Heavenly Father. Amid every trial, He has given me the courage to trust in Him and a level of peace that goes beyond understanding.

I thank God for my husband, Tyrone, who has been my rock. He has shown more patience with me on my journey toward healing than I could have ever imagined. He has been my provider, my protector, my strongest supporter, and my best friend. Thank you for walking with me on this journey.

My children, Crystal, and Lee. I pray this book project will give them a better understanding of my experiences growing up and my unconditional love for them. It is my hope that the lessons learned will give them the courage to heal from their own childhood traumas.

Circumstances can keep us down or lift us up. My parents have taught me to understand the difference. Because of their examples, I can see the best in each circumstance, each challenge I face, and remain strong no matter what. For this I thank them. They have taught me more than they will ever know.

"Sometimes, you can be so full of where you came from that you can't see where you're going."

Pamela Byrd

Table of Contents

INTRODUCTION

"When we experience life's tragedies, we have to make sure we don't miss the message or the assignment that God has for us."

Last year, my twin sister passed away. She took her life. In her mind and in her heart, the only way to sever the emotional ties to her childhood trauma was to end her life. Through this devastating loss, I felt that God was sending me a message I didn't want to miss. He had something He needed me to do. Therefore, I am sharing our story with you.

As I was going through my sister's belongings after she passed away, I stumbled upon her recorded therapy sessions and journals. These treasures allowed me to come face to face with the reality of childhood trauma and the ways it can lead us to make unhealthy decisions. As a result, I am determined to help other women who have been handcuffed to their adverse childhood experiences.

By sharing my experiences and the battles I have overcome growing up in the same highly dysfunctional environment, I am committed to helping others who are dealing with the residual effects of childhood trauma.

Throughout this book, I will be sharing information I have gathered from my sister's possessions. I am taking a bold step by sharing this information candidly with you. But I know that doing so will give you an opportunity to know her better and will provide a much better picture of the struggles she faced than just talking about her would not do.

My sister's strong desire to overcome the emotional damage from her childhood trauma led her to many different therapists over a period of twenty-two years. She recorded many of her therapy sessions as a way of working through their discussions between sessions. I have listened to these recordings and provided my own journaling reflections to share with you. This personal glimpse into her private therapy sessions will reveal her attempts to fight the numerous demons present in her life much better than my mere third-party words can possibly convey. The names will be either changed or omitted in order to protect the privacy of others involved.

As a Christian, my natural tendency is to come to you from a spiritual perspective. Through my relationship with Jesus Christ, I have come to the place where I am able to share our story with you. But there is so much more that needs to be shared. From a psychological and scientific perspective, understanding the numerous ways childhood trauma affects our brains and how we develop into adulthood provides clarity and a sense of relief in knowing that there's nothing wrong with us. We are human, just like everyone else. But our painful childhood experiences have left us handicapped in a way that can't be diagnosed or treated as readily as a physical one might.

You will also gain insight into the path I chose to overcome my own traumatic childhood experiences. The journey has not been easy. The work required to overcome such painful experiences is ongoing and requires a lot of courage. As strange as it may seem, the death of my sister has given me a new level of courage, the courage to share her story in hopes of helping others conquer the demons in their own lives and begin the work towards emotional healing.

NOTE: This book is not intended to be a comprehensive study on childhood trauma from a mental health standpoint, but I would be remiss in not sharing the information I have learned as a result of my own extensive research into the subject of childhood trauma. I have listed several resources at the end of this book that include numerous research articles to further your understanding of the medical research on this topic. My goal is to lay the foundation that supports the experiences I have lived through and the variety of outcomes possible when a child who experienced childhood trauma did not have the care of healthy adults to help them along in their stages of development.

By sharing my experiences and the battles I have overcome growing up in the same highly dysfunctional environment, I am committed to helping others who are dealing with the residual effects of childhood trauma.

As I shine light on the manipulative tactics the enemy uses to keep women in bondage to their painful past, they can begin to sever their own emotional ties. This knowledge gives them the courage they need to re-claim their authentic power.

To get the most from this book, I have divided it into three sections: Trauma, Drama and Mama. These three topics will help you to understand how each role manifests in our lives as a result of our painful childhood experiences. It is up to you to decide if you will allow your painful past to undermine the decisions you make. The more you learn from each section, the more equipped you will be to prevent your own drama from infecting the lives of your children or anyone else that you hold close to your heart.

In order to re-claim your authentic power, you must:

Section 1: Trauma

Acknowledge the trauma you experienced at an age when you had no power to stop it. You had to accept your life and experiences with no power to stop those painful experiences from happening, realizing that your authentic power was taken away from you in those very moments.

Section 2 - Drama

Understand that drama manifests when you act out from the trauma you experienced. When you allow this to happen, you surrender to the enemy's plans to use your trauma against you, to keep you from realizing just how powerful you are as a child of God. Your authentic power is further diminished when you allow drama to play out in the lives of everyone around you.

Section 3 – Mama

Accept that as a mother, future mother, or the caregiver for any child, you must address the experienced trauma before you bring your own children into this world, or before you allow the cycle to repeat itself in the children you have already created or in those who are under your care. If neglected, the generational dysfunction will continue and manifest in behaviors from your offspring that you cannot even imagine.

Before we begin, I must caution you. As I share our story with you, the enemy (Satan) will attempt to do everything within his power to prevent you from embracing the intention of this book. I bring him to the forefront to impress upon you the importance of staying focused on how you process the information I am sharing with you. Someone once implied to me that I should not focus so much attention on the enemy. If you don't know your enemy and how he operates, how can you defeat him?

Let us begin.

TRAUMA

CHAPTER 1

THE ORIGIN OF TRAUMA

Broken

> Reading from In Touch magazine August, 99: God has a solution for the tensions and pressures we face. He knows our longing for peace and safety, and He has promised to provide both for us.
>
> How do I long for something I've never known? I don't think I've ever known peace and safety, calmness, comfort, a sense of well-being. God knows the desires of our hearts. Is peace and safety the secret desire of my heart? What a question. Everyone wants that, yeah, but long for it. I have no idea what I long for. I long for death.
>
> Journal Entry, My Twin

If you ever experienced any form of abuse as a child, you experienced childhood trauma. Even if two children experience the same type of trauma, they may not be affected the same way. Scientists tell us that some children develop resilience or the ability to overcome significant trauma, while others do not.

The American Psychological Association (APA) has defined trauma as some emotional or psychological response to a horrific event. Abuse constitutes a horrific event. Forms of abuse include physical, sexual, emotional, psychological, or religious. Other forms of abuse include neglect, losing a parent, either through death, abandonment, or divorce. A child may have had a parent in jail, may have been exposed to physical violence, or witnessed a household member with an addiction to drugs or alcohol.

This is what I refer to as collateral damage, when our traumatic childhood experiences adversely affect our future decision making. We tend to make unhealthy decisions based on the ways we internalized our childhood trauma. The problem with this behavior is that it affects us and everyone within our circle.

Let me bring this closer to home for more clarity. Have you ever mopped your kitchen floor and accidentally knocked over the bucket of dirty water? The spillage is never confined to the space where it fell. It pours out and flows all over the floor. This dirty water knows no boundaries. It seeps into every crack and crevice at an accelerated pace and has the authority to damage anything it touches. This is what happens when our painful experiences spill over into other areas of our lives. The dirty wounds begin to touch all our relationships and soak into them like damaged carpet from a broken water pipe.

If you experienced any form of childhood trauma and did not have a healthy adult to support, nurture, or provide a safe environment for you, you may experience toxic stress. Scientists have proven that early childhood experiences play a large role in the way the brain develops and functions. I will go into more detail about these findings in the next chapter.

I grew up in a horrendous environment of dysfunction. This dysfunction was passed down to my generation like a baton passed to a sprint runner in a relay race. Three batons were handed down from my parents to me and my two sisters. We each grabbed our own designated batons quite innocently. We each believed our baton was safe, something we could hold onto for dear life. We each believed that these batons were the tools we needed to run this race called life. Two of us grew weary. Consequently, both of my sisters bowed out of the race and transitioned into the arms of our heavenly Father. I alone have been charged to finish this race. I have paused in this race long enough to grab the batons from both of my sisters as I strive to finish this race for them, a race that gives meaning to their existence, to help other women heal from their childhood wounds and reclaim their authentic power. This power they need to pass the baton to their children so they can hold securely to their own authentic power.

If you have experienced any level of trauma as a child, it has manifested in one way or another. It may not be evident to others because you've learned to hide it well from plain sight. You've been able to wear a mask that others don't know about.

There may be faint glimpses. When your trauma is triggered by a particular experience, there might be just a flicker of curiosity from outsiders wondering, "what just happened?". They can't put their fingers on it, but they know that something is "off". I have Tourette syndrome, a neurological disorder that manifests in "tics". People may know I have it, or they may not, depending on how long they are around me. But from a relational distance, they may not know unless they've spent a lot of time around me.

Then, there are those whose childhood trauma may be so evident that people can see it from a mile away. It may not be identified as childhood trauma to the untrained eye, but others know that something's just not right. What happens in these situations is people who do not understand the manifestations of childhood trauma will either criticize the victims, pass judgement against them, gossip about them, or simply distance themselves altogether.

Let us not leave out those who have unresolved childhood trauma and have learned to manipulate you. Then, through your own lack of awareness, you internalize their manipulative behavior. This only continues to diminish any authentic power you happened to hold onto from your damaged childhood.

This is what happened to me and my sisters. Our authentic power was stripped away from us as children. This power continued to get depleted from each of us throughout our lives. Our story paints a picture of what happens when children who suffer from abuse are not given the emotional support needed from adults. This nurturing component is crucial in determining how well children will adjust to their adverse childhood experiences as adults.

My older sister was diagnosed with a weak heart when she became pregnant with her only daughter at the age of 35. The doctors informed her that she would not live a long life as a result of her heart problems and would need to take precautions. She had a massive stroke seven years later and died a year after that at the age of 43. During that eight-year period, she was supplied with regular amounts of cocaine and marijuana by a family member. These drugs weakened her heart and led to her death.

My twin sister took her own life as a result of the trauma she experienced in childhood. She suffered ongoing bouts of depression and attempted suicide numerous times. Eight months before her passing, her husband was diagnosed with terminal cancer. She was his sole caregiver. She struggled physically, emotionally and mentally while caring for him. I traveled to their home several times during that eight-month period to help relieve some of the stress this situation brought on for the two of them. As is common with most cancer patients, her husband was prescribed opioid drugs for his pain. In a desperate effort to numb her own emotional pain, my sister formed an addiction to his pain medications. She used these pain medications to end her life.

Now, I will stop here for a moment to explain something. My sister and I were not identical twins, but we were extremely close. After her death, people have often asked me, "What made the two of you so different, given the fact that you grew up in the same dysfunctional environment?" We weren't that different, at all. We just chose to walk different paths. My sister chose to cling to the hope of love from our mother and absent father. Now, there is nothing wrong with the choice she made. We all yearn to be loved by our parents in a healthy way. I, on the other hand, accepted the absence of love and sought to find it outside of the home. As you might say, I looked in all the wrong places, desperately seeking to find the love that I never experienced at home.

As I look back over each of our lives, the three of us, I can see how God had his hands on each of us. Most importantly, I believe that God has given me a mandate. That mandate is to stand in the gap for those women whom the enemy has manipulated into believing that they have no power against the forces that hold them in bondage to their past.

God has used the deaths of my two sisters to remind me of my own spiritual gifts and the reason for them. He has reminded me of my own authentic power, that which was taken away from me as a little girl. Now, I can help other women to heal from their own childhood trauma. I have done the work. I have sought after the Lord to equip me to do His work. But first, I needed to get clear on my identity as a child of God. I had to face the demons trying to hold me captive to my childhood trauma.

One of the major differences between the path I chose and that my sister chose is that because of her yearning to receive that love from our parents, specifically our mother, she placed herself in a position to be emotionally and mentally abused by her for the remainder of her life. I, on the other hand, chose to distance myself for my own emotional health and safety.

> "We cannot get to the place where we are emotionally and mentally healthy if we continue to stay in the same environment that created the trauma." (Karen Casey) [1]

Author Karen Casey has written numerous books on Detachment. Detaching from toxic relationships and distancing yourself from toxic relationships helps you to remain safe as you work towards your healing.

You Can Tell a Lot about a Woman by Her Choice of Undergarments

At this point, you may be thinking, "I have experienced some form of trauma as a child, but it doesn't affect who I am today." Are you sure about that?

I was brought up to appreciate undergarments. The right bra can make or break an outfit. There are different types of bras for different styles of clothing. There are undergarments that smooth and define. There are undergarments that hide parts that others should never see.

Bear with me, I bring this up to make a point.

While out shopping the other day, I passed by a woman wearing a cute form fitting dress, walking to her car. At first glance, I could see that her bra was too small. Her breasts were spilling out the sides of her bra. Her bra was not providing the support her breasts needed. This did not give her a polished look or do any justice to her dress. I believe that at one time in her life, this bra fit. Whether she grew out of it, or whether the bra was worn out, it made a difference in the dress she wore and how she looked in it.

You can spend all the money in the world on the fanciest wardrobe, but if you don't invest in the right undergarments, your outer garment will not look as beautiful on you as you imagined it would when you purchased it. The investment you make in the garments you wear underneath will ensure a smooth, polished look on the outside. If we fail to do a periodic assessment of our undergarments, we may not realize the negative impact they have on our outward appearance.

As adults who have experienced childhood trauma, we can put on a garment of confidence. We can be highly educated, have a beautiful home, drive an expensive car and have a social media profile that rivals any lifestyle celebrity, but if we have somehow shoved our painful experiences into a box and buried them somewhere deep inside of us, like our breasts in a worn-out bra, we have no idea how our wounds are impacting our lives and showing up in our current experiences. As a result, the garment we want others to see, that garment of confidence, might not be what others see at all.

No matter how much we try to keep those painful memories buried, if we aren't investing in our own healing from these painful experiences, our inner turmoil somehow surfaces and minimizes the beauty of what others see on the outside, no matter how much we try to hide them.

Every woman should own at least one full length mirror. This is an essential item for every stage of life. Even better, a full-length trifold mirror that gives her an opportunity to see what she may not readily see without it. This panoramic view tells her what is working in a particular choice of clothing and what is not. It can give her a full picture of an outfit to determine what looks best on her.

This book is meant to provide a different kind of full body mirror, a panoramic view of who you are and how you came to be at the place where you are right now. This full view gives you a chance to discover how your past traumas may be influencing the choices you make, the disappointments you experience, and the conflict that arises from behaviors you may not even be aware of. This mirror will also provide answers to the questions you may have about your experiences that leave you with feelings of confusion, frustration and hopelessness.

Are You Ready To Look in The Mirror?

As a Life Coach, I generally work with women who know they need to set healthy boundaries but are not sure how to set them. Their inability to set needed boundaries usually stems from their childhood experiences. Once they discover the connection between their childhood experiences and their current situation, they are better equipped to set needed boundaries.

After my sister's death, God prompted me to consider working with women who have experienced childhood trauma who have yet to bear children to help them understand that no child should come into this world and deal with the pain of childhood trauma inflicted upon them by mothers or fathers, for that matter, who failed to deal with their own childhood trauma. The cycle must be broken.

Unfortunately, I didn't learn this lesson in time. I passed the baton to my own children. Before I began my healing process, I created collateral damage that my children must now work through. It wasn't until my son reported me for child abuse when he was 11 years old that I was court-ordered to attend parenting classes. While the case of abuse was "unfounded", I can honestly say that this court order was the best thing that ever happened to me. I realized, for the first time, that the foundation had been laid in raising my own children. This foundation of learned dysfunctional behavior was damaging their emotional well-being. I had no idea that the way I was raised was wrong. It was all I knew, so I continued this pattern of dysfunction, spewing toxic residue all over my children.

I still suffer the consequences of my behavior. The damage has been done, but I pray every day that my relationship with my children will be restored. I have asked them both for forgiveness. Now, I allow God to work in their lives. They are adults now. It will be up to them to seek the healing they need. In the meantime, I continue to set the example, using my authentic power to speak to those who have had their power taken away from them through no fault of their own. I continue to be the warrior God has created me to be, to fight for those who are victims, letting them know that they don't have to remain victims to their past. They can stand up, do the work of healing and regain their authentic power before that damage manifests in the lives of their children.

Whether you have children or are considering having children in the future, and you've experienced childhood trauma at a time when you were unable to speak up for yourself, decide to DO THE WORK. Not only for you, but for them. That precious little boy or girl should not have to deal with the trauma that little girl inside you had to endure. I don't think there's a bone in your body that would want to inflict that pain on another precious child of God, especially one you love.

Reach out to your Heavenly Father. Have a heart-to-heart with

Him. Let Him know what you need. He'll be there for you. As you go through the arduous process of healing, He will be with you. At times, He will even carry you. Allow Him to reveal to you the reason you are here and the reason for your pain so you can heal, if not for you, then for those whom God has entrusted to you. This journey will not be a short one, but it will be worth it. You are worth it, and so are your children. Do it for you. Do it for them. Do it so that you are able to carry out God's call for your life, so, you can begin using the spiritual gifts that He has given you. Only then, will you begin to understand how to use those gifts to impact the lives of His children and His kingdom.

My Journal Entry 3/28/2021

My sister has been gone a week now. She took her life last Friday or Saturday. She was found dead in her home on Saturday evening. This is the first time I am journaling since these events took place. This is the first time I have had a chance to sit back and really assess where I am with all of this. I have lost my twin sister. I am deeply saddened and experiencing a wide range of emotions, but mostly sadness.

It's true, no one can tell you anything about your grief. No one really understands the person you lost the way you do. Sorrow is so different. My tears are different now. The pain is like nothing I've experienced before. I believe with my whole heart that she is happy now with our sister and our grandmother, two people she loved so dearly. I believe she is finally at peace.

Never have I been so sure of helping women to set the right boundaries as I am now after her death. Realizing all that she endured for all these years, all the pain. She was living in a hell, and I couldn't do anything about it. Oh, I tried, but ultimately, she had to decide what she would do about it. I do feel bad that I was just there with her, and I didn't acknowledge the signs. But, given her inability to make a decision that would cause others to be angry with her, she chose to be angry with herself instead.

Where Was God?

Before we go any further, I want to help answer this question. Many have blamed God for their horrible childhood experiences. They have even questioned how God can let something like this happen to them.

To be honest, I have questioned God myself. Why did he place me in this life, in this family, to experience the horrible things I have experienced? I knew there had to be a reason, and there had to be answers, so I sought after them. I didn't just sit back and exclaim, "Woe is me!" I couldn't imagine going through life living in fear of what life would bring next or remaining angry at someone I knew nothing about. So, what did I do? I went straight to the source. I went to God. He and I have crucial conversations, and I listen. I don't just talk. I listen. Our conversations have led me to a greater understanding of Him. His guidance has helped me to know more about His love for me from a much broader perspective.

When I attempt to find answers based on the world, I find none. But when I peer through the lens of God's omnipotence, I see a much broader picture. When I go to Him, He allows me to see through that amazing lens. As I continue to look deeper, I realize that I have an assignment. For me to complete my assignment, I must trust God's plan. I believe I was placed on this earth to impact lives, but I can't impact the lives of others in a powerful way until I accept the experiences I have had as necessary to complete the assignment He has for me, the assignment He is equipping me to fulfill.

God's Word offers many examples of people who have experienced trauma much worse than mine or yours.

Joseph's brothers plotted to kill him by throwing him in a pit but then chose to sell him to the Ishmaelites for twenty pieces of silver, the ultimate account of sibling jealousy and rivalry (Genesis 18:30)

Abraham was about to sacrifice his beloved son as a result of God's instruction (Genesis 22:1-13).

Moses had to flee the only land he knew at the age of 40 and wander in the dessert for 40 years. Imagine the plight he had to experience during those years (Exodus 2).

As their stories unfold, we can see the bigger picture and how each of their lives have made it possible for us to live the lives we live right now. Why should we be any different?

> "Trust in the Lord with all your heart and lean not on your own understanding; in ALL your ways, acknowledge Him, and He shall direct your paths "(Proverbs 3:5-6).

These are probably two of the most universally referenced verses in the bible, at least within the book of Proverbs, but have you really taken the time to understand what this really means?

Don't ask why, unless, of course, you are questioning your own actions. Are you trusting, leaning and relying on Him – in ALL things? If not, that's probably why you're questioning. If not, my question is WHY NOT?

Could there be something you are doing or not doing that is causing you to not know, recognize and consequently not acknowledge Him? These are the things that guarantee He will direct and make straight your paths.

God is not out there to confuse us. There is too much confusion in this world. He's out to make our paths straight and to give us peace and joy. It's up to us to make sure that we are doing our part to obtain it. When you are doing this, you experience that joy that goes beyond understanding.

> "Happy is the man who finds wisdom, and the man who gains understanding." (Proverbs 3:13).

Each of your life experiences is necessary, and your pursuit of wisdom helps you to use these experiences in a way that brings glory to Him!

I love to use the example of Helen Keller. Caroline Myss wrote a book entitled Sacred Contracts[2] which helps to explain how God assigns each of us to fulfill something here on this earth, and she shares this wonderful perspective; had Helen Keller not experienced her life the way she did, had she not been stricken with what was then diagnosed as brain fever and left both blind and deaf at 19 months old, she would never have made the impact that she did. Nelson Mandela, look at what he went through for the nation of South Africa. What we go through is not about us, but sadly we get caught up in "US" instead of seeking to understand the reason we go through what we go through and who will be better off because we lived.

We get so caught up in our own misery without considering God's bigger picture. We all need this reminder, which is why it's so important to spend time with God and read His Word EVERY SINGLE DAY! Even if just for ten minutes. He just gave us another day, the least we can give Him is ten minutes!

You may be angry, you may be bitter, and you may be disappointed, but how well do you really know God? What clarity has He given you? I ask you to seek His answers. Let Him reveal your assignment to you. We have all been placed on this earth for a reason, to fulfill a particular assignment. In order to complete our assignment, there are situations we must go through. Whatever we go through, know that God will be there to give us the courage we need to go through it. We simply must ask Him.

Now that I've gotten that off my chest, let's look at how your painful childhood experiences may be tied to your current reality.

SUMMARY

- **When children experience any type of trauma, they may suffer from adverse effects for the rest of their lives.**

  What adverse effects have you experienced because of your traumas? ______________________________

  ____

  ____

- **Even if two children experience the same type of trauma, they may not be affected the same way.**

- **Collateral damage occurs when our traumatic childhood experiences adversely affect our future decision making.**

  *How has your past influenced your decision making?*_____

  ____

  ____

  ____

- **We tend to make unhealthy decisions based on how we internalized our childhood trauma.**

- **If you experienced any form of childhood trauma and did not have a healthy adult to support, nurture, or provide a safe environment for you, you may experience toxic stress.**

  What type of support did you get to support and nurture you and how has this influenced the way you view your childhood traumas? ______________________________

  ____

  ____

  ____

- **Scientists have proven that early childhood experiences play a large role in the way the brain develops and functions.**

  Which part of this research helps you the most? __________

  ____

  ____

  ____

- Distancing or detaching yourself from toxic relationships helps you to remain safe as you work towards your healing.

  What toxic relationships are you holding onto? How do you feel about distancing and detaching yourself from those toxic relationships? ______________________________

  ____

  ____

- The cycle must be broken

  What is the first thought that comes to mind when you hear that the cycle must be broken? ______________________

  ____
  ____
  ____
  ____
  ____
  ____
  ____
  ____

- Whether you have children or are considering having children in the future and you've experienced childhood trauma at a time when you were unable to speak up for yourself, decide to DO THE WORK.

  How does this statement speak to you? ________________

  ____
  ____
  ____
  ____
  ____
  ____
  ____
  ____
  ____

CHAPTER 2

THE TIES TO OUR CHILDHOOD TRAUMA

Tied in Knots

> Lord, please use what I am learning to free me from those events in the past that keep me from attaching to you and to other people the way I want to. I pray in Jesus' Name. Amen.
>
> Journal Entry, My Twin

Do you remember having a security blanket? Have you ever known a baby or a toddler who cried when denied access to their own security blanket? It may have been a doll, a pillow, or a plush toy. Whichever the case may be, it was a symbol of safety and comfort.

A security blanket is referred to as a transitional object, a safe passage for transitioning from Mommy and Daddy and a growing independence in the world. According to an article in the Huffington Post, a security blanket can offer a safe way to transition from dependence to independence. When a child fails to allow the transition and holds on to his security blanket, it can cause an unhealthy dependence and a delay in a child's ability to become independent from their parents.

Sometimes, we may treat our painful childhood experiences (*ACE*

– aka adverse childhood experiences) like that security blanket. We create such a bond to that trauma that we never want to let it go. Our fear of letting go of the trauma can cause us to hold on even more tightly, so tightly that we create a knot to bind it to us, making it extremely difficult to break free from it. The longer we hold on, the tighter the knot gets. Whether we realize it or not, an unhealthy dependence on our trauma will influence how we live our lives. When we hold fast to the painful memories of our tattered youth experiences like a two-year-old holding tight to a worn but favorite security blanket, we deprive ourselves of the lessons we could learn as a result of them.

When my sister passed away, I needed answers. I didn't want to leave any stone unturned as to what drove her to take her own life. My quest led me to discover the connection between childhood trauma and the brain. The medical information I gathered was mind boggling. My initial response to the research I conducted was disappointment. I was disappointed with myself for not taking the time to do this research years earlier. I could have eliminated so many of the mistakes I made had I only understood the effects of childhood trauma on the brain. Then I began to feel guilty. If only I had done this research earlier, I could have prevented my sister from taking her life.

> "Now this is the confidence that we have in Him, that if we ask anything according to His will, He hears us. And if we know that He hears us, whatever we ask, we know that we have the petitions that we have asked of Him" (1 John 5:14-15).

After realizing that the enemy was planting these thoughts

in my head, I began to pray. This gave me a much healthier perspective. As I considered the brain's response to childhood trauma, I came to a better understanding of why my sister took her life. She was worn down. Her level of depression impacted her emotional state. As a result, her cognitive state had grown weary and overloaded, incapable of handling all that weighed heavily upon her. It had all become too much to carry. It was as if someone were piling bowling balls in her arms to hold onto. Eventually, they became so heavy that she had to drop them. Not that she chose to drop them, but they became so heavy she had no choice but to drop them.

Trauma and Your Brain

As I indicated earlier, my goal is to provide spiritual as well as scientific insights that will further your understanding of childhood trauma, to let you rest, knowing that "you're not crazy". There is an explanation for the feelings you feel and your tendency to respond the way you do in certain situations. Using the information I have gathered, I will share statistics on how our brains respond to trauma. My hope is that it will give you a higher level of understanding about the long-term effects of childhood trauma.

Adverse Childhood Experiences (aka ACE) are stresses or traumatic events that children experience before age 18. Studies have linked exposure to ACEs and negative health to developmental and behavioral outcomes.[3]

Over 50% of adolescents have been exposed to ACEs. This

exposure can have detrimental effects on learning and behavior and is associated with increased suicidal ideation in adolescents.

ACEs have a different impact on the brain, based on the age of exposure, individual factors and microsystem protective factors.

ACEs contribute to disturbances in cognitive and affective processes including:

- Heightened attention toward threatening stimuli
- Increased experience of loneliness
- Reduced impulse control
- Functional alterations in key stress and emotion associated brain regions, particularly the anterior cingulate cortex [AGG], amygdala and hippocampus (shrinkage)
- Initial increase in amygdala volume after ACEs followed by a decrease in volume due to persistent stress in later life
- Exposure to specific types of traumas selectively affect the sensory systems involved in perceiving the trauma

I know this all sounds like a lot of scientific mumbo jumbo to the medically untrained ear. Let me see if I can make sense of this information for you based on my own understanding.

Trauma occurs when someone is overwhelmed by something that is out of their control. When we experience trauma, our brains respond in one of three different ways, depending on the type of trauma; fight, flight, or freeze.

There is a part of our brain (the hippocampus) that files memories. But at the time of trauma, it stops filing memories and diverts to pumping a stress hormone called cortisol in our bodies. This helps, because it causes us to stop focusing on our pain so we can focus on survival. Imagine someone in war losing a limb and being able to carry that limb with them to a place of safety. They stop feeling the pain long enough to survive. This is our bodies' way of protecting us. When we experience trauma, the survival brain takes over the rational brain.

An interesting thing about the hippocampus is that while it is responsible for holding memories, it holds painful memories more than pleasurable memories. My sister would often share experiences with me from our childhood that were deemed pleasurable. I wouldn't remember them. But when she brought up a painful memory, I remembered it quite vividly. This was one of the differences between how her brain processed memories and mine. This is how we begin to develop patterns of behavior that impact our lives as adults. Here's a great example of that, one that I just recently discovered through my research.

When trauma events happen, our brains decide how they will respond. My sister was extremely nurturing. Her immediate response to trauma was to freeze. Because we remained in the home, she would do whatever she could to care for the abuser. Her hope was that if she "cared" enough, she could prevent the abuse from happening again. On the other hand, I would flee. As adults, my sister and I handled our stress from trauma differently. When she experienced stressful situations that triggered her early childhood trauma, she would freeze. She would stay in the situation, not knowing how to escape it. When I experienced a stressful situation that triggered my childhood trauma, I would flee. This made it very easy for me to leave a situation rather than stay in the pain. Both responses were unhealthy forms of dealing with our trauma.

Three Types of Traumas[4]

There are three main types of traumas that differ based on what caused them and how they are manifested.

Acute Trauma

This kind of trauma is caused by a single traumatic event. The events are usually very distressing and dangerous for the patient's mental health and are not universal for everyone. A few examples of acute trauma are rape, child molestation or witnessing a heinous crime. The person's physical as well as emotional security is threatened by the event, and they can respond in different ways.

Chronic Trauma

Chronic Trauma is a result of a series of highly depressing and stressful events that can be connected but do not have to be. An example of chronic trauma is sexual abuse. Acute trauma can develop into chronic trauma if not taken care of properly and on time.

Complex Trauma

Complex trauma is usually a product of long exposure to disturbing events that happen at a young age. Most of the time, children and young adults are the victims of this culprit. When children are not protected and taken care of by their parents as they should be, they get hurt by it and because of it. This trauma can have a long-term effect on their mental health and lives in general. Any form of sexual abuse that continues over a period of years would be considered a form of complex trauma.

Any form of trauma can result in secondary PTSD or post-traumatic stress disorder. This form of PTSD can last for years. A continuous increase in our levels of cortisol in our bloodstream increases our ability to remember painful memories long after the experiences have passed. These memories can also be triggered by anything, a color, a smell, a sound, a sensation. We will delve deeper into triggers in the next chapter.

Taking Back What Was Taken Away

If you experienced any form of trauma as a child, something precious has been taken away from you. Your dignity, your joy, your happiness and your self-worth, just to name a few. The painful memories we hold onto rob us of the opportunity to live the life we so dreamed of as innocent, precious children. Your innocence was taken away from you. While you may never get back your innocence, you can take back your power by understanding how those painful experiences have shaped you and how to thrive in spite of them. No matter what happened, they cannot take away your identity. As you come to terms with your true identity, who God created you to be, you can begin to reclaim your authentic power.

I hope you are beginning to realize how important it is to focus on processing your painful childhood experiences. Your willingness to address your past shows courage. It is this courage that will help you to reclaim your authentic power.

What is Authentic Power?

Authentic power is the internal power you possess, the power that has been inside you all along. This power is so real that it can vibrate to the core of your very being. It is who you are and reveals who you were created to be.

Oftentimes, the power we possess as women is minimized when we begin to believe the lies that the enemy has told us for so long,

> You're not pretty enough, you're not strong enough, you're too this, or you're too that or even you're not this, or you're not that.

When we hear these types of self-deprecating statements repeatedly, we begin to internalize them. These statements can come from our parents, peers or even strangers. Even worse, they can come from the lies we tell ourselves based on our past hurts. These lies cause our sense of power to be blown away like the lit candles blown out on a birthday cake.

This is a strategy that the enemy has used against us since the beginning of time, a strategy that distracts us from realizing just how amazing we truly are. Why? Because if he can distract us with these false beliefs about ourselves, he can throw us off course from our intended destination, that place where God wants us to be.

Because I grew up in a highly dysfunctional environment in a single parent home, I was determined to bypass the destination that many had pre-determined I would follow. To those unaware of the trauma that was taking place in our home, I was destined to be a failure. By all accounts, it was a foregone conclusion that I would become pregnant at an early age and continue the pattern that was set before me.

> I'm convinced Pam was hurting and was looking for someone to love her and unfortunately, she was used by boys and men in pursuit of love. She didn't feel loved by our mother. And our father, he was just a man who shared our blood but knew nothing about us. He took no initiative to know us even though he lived in the same state.
>
> Journal Entry, My Twin

Through my determination to change my pre-conceived outcome, I discovered supernatural forces trying to keep me away from my destiny. Had I not gathered the knowledge I needed and utilized the tools that were available to me to change the course of my presumed destiny despite my behavior, I would have allowed the enemy to win. I was crying out, and God heard my cry.

The Journey toward Healing

As we begin the process of severing the emotional ties to our childhood trauma, as we move toward letting go–not forgetting but letting go, we must first look at our experiences from a place of curiosity through childlike faith. We must be willing to excavate the origin of these memories and relocate them to a secure platform for further examination.

Have you ever searched for anything, found it, and brought it inside or outside, placed it under a light, in clear view so that you could get a closer look at it? I remember looking for a box of family photos in my garage. When I finally reached it among the stacked, cobweb drenched boxes, I proceeded to take it into the house, dust it off and place it on the kitchen table. This gave me a chance to view them in a different light where I had a better view. I spread the photographs out on the table and observed the intricate detail of each still capture. Each picture took me back to that time and place. I began to reflect on what occurred during that time. Just seeing the picture was not enough. I had to intentionally transport myself back to that time like a well-calibrated time machine. This journey back in time allowed me to remember experiences I had completely forgotten. The picture came to life and gave me a live, panoramic view of where I was at that given place in time.

Because of our travels through our adolescence and our entry into adulthood, our experiences have accumulated and made us who we are. Our frames of reference are now more expansive and allow us to see things more clearly, that is if we are open and willing to do so. When we come to that place of examination, we gain a better understanding of who we are and how we came to be the gifted individuals we are. When we acknowledge (and celebrate) our willingness to remain open, we are then at a higher level of maturity, a level of maturity where we allow ourselves to spread everything out on the table. Once there, we can discover lessons learned as a result of how far we have come.

Even though my sisters and I grew up in the same environment and had about 90% of the same experiences within the home, we took different routes as it relates to how we internalized our experiences. My twin sister positioned herself within the victim role, while I took a lot of risks by trying to step out of the environment, seeking some other type of relief from the pain. Many of the decisions I made led me into another type of pain, but at least I was searching outside. I had to muster the courage to get to another place, outside of my environment. I was determined to escape the pain of my reality. I refused to remain a victim. Even though I did whatever I could to escape physically, I carried victim behavior with me for many years. It wasn't until I came face to face with the reality of my "victimhood" that I was able to change my behavior and create desired outcomes.

How do you know if you're still playing the role of victim long after the traumatic event has passed?

How have your adverse childhood experiences dictated the decisions you make now?

How will these experiences create your outcome?

Are you unsure of how your experiences are influencing your current reality?

These are extremely difficult questions to answer. Most of my answers didn't come until someone had the courage to ask them of me. To answer them, I had to realize that I was holding onto self-sabotaging beliefs. These false beliefs were preventing me from seeing the reality of my own victimhood.

Until you're ready to come face to face with how you have internalized those painful experiences, you may never know. I am that someone who has the courage to ask you these questions. Do you have the courage to answer them?

There Is No Joy in Victimhood

Victimization is something that we all experience as human beings. We all fall into the role of victim at some point in our lives. We often fall victim to the actions of others or the circumstances in which we find ourselves that are beyond our control. We may have been the victim of a crime: a break-in, a rape, a molestation, or an attack of some form. These are all circumstances where we are legitimately considered victims. Any situation that violates our freedom to govern our bodies and our lifestyle choice can place us in the victim position. The terrorist attack on 9/11/2001 against the United States of America indoctrinated many victims: not only those who died, but the families and friends of those who were left to grieve the loss of these individuals. Our country fell victim to this horrific attack as well as many other countries that were devastated by this extreme act of hate and violation of our freedom.

Victimization vs. Victimhood

There is a vast difference between victimization and victimhood. When we have been victimized, as the examples given above, we can accept our role as victims and seek ways to heal in order to move beyond the pain of the hurt that accompanies such violations, or we can choose to allow these circumstances and experiences to define us and hold us hostage.

Victimhood is when we emphasize our "poor me" message and allow it to serve as an expression of who we are. Victimhood is an identity that many will deny. It's not until we consider these two definitions that we can begin to identify how we have internalized our painful experiences and begin to consider the behaviors we exhibit as a result.

We can get so comfortable in our role as victims that any threat of moving us out of it will cause us to immediately take a defensive position. "But you don't know what I've been through!" This reaction to a perceived interruption of our victim role translates into victimhood. When we choose to hold onto our painful experiences, our non-verbal reaction toward a perceived "accuser" can be either retaliation through the silent treatment, revenge, or a reminder of the "accuser's" past mistakes. These are all ploys to transfer guilt, deny or justify our own behavior. If we succeed with any of these tactics, we can then take a leisurely stroll back to the victim position and settle into our comfortable recliner of victimhood once again. But how much joy is there in that position?

Any time we find ourselves complaining, we are in the victim role. While we all find ourselves in the position of "victim" from time to time, we do have the choice of moving beyond victimhood.

The Matter of Choice

Through every adversity, you have a choice. You can either learn from it and become an inspiration for others, or you can remain victim to it and cause an avalanche of destruction all around you. It is totally up to you. You decide.

In the next section of this book, we will look at ways your adverse childhood experiences could be influencing where you are now: physically, emotionally, and spiritually.

How do you prevent them from sabotaging your relationships?

How have your past experiences spilled over into your relationships with others, family, co-workers, friends, significant others?

Most importantly, how has your interpretation of these experiences helped or hindered you from having a better understanding of who you are?

How can you take this information and use it to re-claim your authentic power?

Excerpt from my journal entries:

> *I believe much of my sister's brokenness stemmed from the day she was held back in kindergarten. She was judged and condemned by our mother when she was held back. Our mother's response was to make my sister feel like a failure. She was yelled at and criticized repeatedly for having to repeat kindergarten all over again. This*

is one of the reasons why my sister was overly fearful about making others angry. She knew how it felt when someone was angry with her. My sister's subsequent conversations with my mother revealed that this decision to hold her back and have her repeat kindergarten was a way to prevent her and me from being so close. I know that this decision caused her to feel inadequate and caused her to seek perfection. In school, she worked hard to get straight A's. She did everything she could to please our mother, even taking care of her when she came home drunk and suffered from a hangover in the morning. My sister would warm up a can of chicken noodle soup with just the right amount of water. She served her soup, saltine crackers, a tall glass of cold milk and two pain relief tablets in bed to help her recover from her hangover.

I listened to a couple of my sister's recorded therapy sessions. It was important to discover that as an adult, the reason she didn't stop talking to our mother was because she was afraid of her. The fear that had been instilled in her was psychologically paralyzing and kept her in the freeze position for the rest of her life.

SUMMARY

- Trauma occurs when someone is overwhelmed by something that is out of their control.

  Now that you understand the neurological aspects of trauma, how does it relate to you? ______________________________

  ____
  ____
  ____
  ____
  ____
  ____
  ____

- The three main forms of trauma include acute trauma, chronic trauma and complex trauma

  Which form(s) of trauma have you experienced? __________

  ____
  ____
  ____
  ____
  ____
  ____
  ____

• Any form of trauma can result in secondary PTSD or post-traumatic stress disorder. This form of PTSD can last for years.

Which form(s) of trauma have you experienced? ________

____

____

____

____

____

• An unhealthy dependence on our trauma will influence how we live our lives.

How true is this statement for you? ________________

____

____

____

____

____

• The power we possess as women is minimized when we begin to believe the lies that the enemy has told us for so long.

What lies have you held onto for far too long? __________

____

____

____

____

- As we begin the process of severing the emotional ties to our childhood trauma, we must be willing to excavate the origin of our painful memories and relocate them to a secure platform for further examination.

  How willing are you to address the origin of your painful memories? ______________________________

  ____

  ____

  ____

  ____

  ____

  ____

  ____

- Once we understand the difference between victimization and victimhood, we can identify how we have internalized our painful experiences and consider the behaviors we exhibit as a result.

  In which category do you fall into and why? ____________

  ____

  ____

  ____

  ____

  ____

  ____

  ____

DRAMA

CHAPTER 3
ALL GROWN UP

Let's step back for a moment and consider how your life would be different if you recognized the impact of trauma in your own life. What would you be doing now? Me? I would be a lawyer or a psychotherapist. I would be the owner of a well-established business and market motivational items for people to display in their homes and offices.

These professions are the dreams I wrote about in my diaries as a young girl and in my journals throughout my twenties. What were your dreams? Will you allow yourself a few moments to think about your childhood dreams? How did you picture your life?

When Life Gets in The Way

What choices did you make that altered that path? Could it be that the path you dreamed of was not based on your plans but on God's plan? People say quite lightheartedly, "We make plans, and God laughs at them." This is not to make light of our plights, but a way of accepting that our plan is not always God's plan for our lives. God's plan has always been for us to impact the lives of others in a way that shines light on His glory. When you think of the dreams you had as a little girl, what result did you see yourself attaining?

When I dreamt of being a lawyer, it was to help people who were limited in their capacity to fight for themselves, to be their voices.

When I dreamt of becoming a psychotherapist, it was to help people to make sense of their pain and live more peaceful lives. When I dreamt of owning a motivational item business, it was to provide a daily perspective of how beautiful life can be when we take the time to see the wonderful possibilities all around us.

Isn't it interesting that the dreams I had so long ago are being manifested in this very moment? His plans are not my plans, but He takes all the gifts He has given me, all the desires of my heart, and creates a beautiful rendition of all I have ever dreamed of. Oh, it didn't happen in the way I had envisioned, but trust me, God knows what He is doing!

Can you see how God is using your dreams and painful experiences to create a beautiful masterpiece in you? If we focus on our pain and disappointments, we miss out on seeing the beauty that transpires as a result. Only God can bring us to such a place of peace and joy. Our revelations of the plans He has for us can be found when we step back long enough to look at what He has done in our lives.

Believe it or not, it's never too late to right a wrong. It's never too late to admit we were unaware of how our own pain has impacted our lives and the decisions we have made. Now is an ideal time to consider how our decisions have impacted others.

My experiences have been painful. The roads I have traveled have not been paved with freshly poured asphalt. They have been quite rocky. Every detour has taken me to another opportunity to grow into who He needs me to be. No matter where the road is taking you, you are never at an impasse. You are not stuck. It may seem that you have reached a dead end, but God has already made a way. You simply must go to Him for direction. Take a moment right now and ask God, "Where are you leading me?" If your past decisions have brought you to where you are at this very moment (and they have), ask Him to give you the spiritual insight to discern what you are now able to do to give Him the glory.

I searched and searched for meaning behind my sister's death. It wasn't until I began to search for reasons beyond what I knew that I was able to gain peace. It wasn't until I began to consider a picture so much larger than what I could see through my own vision, that I understood how God was making a way for my gifts to manifest.

It's hard to understand God's plan for our lives, based on our limited human point of view. I recently had a conversation with God in my journal. In my written conversations with God, I use a particular journaling style called Dialogical. This advanced journaling style gives me a wonderful opportunity to gain a higher level of spiritual clarity. Allow me to share this conversation with you.

My Journal Entry

I am feeling remorseful about the way I handled my sister and my brother-in-law in their final days. I am beginning to feel guilty in that I didn't do everything I should have done. I didn't follow my heart. I didn't take time to listen to the Holy Spirit. I proceeded with allowing someone to dictate what I did during the most crucial time of their lives. I just prayed to God, asking Him to forgive me for not listening and heeding His direction instead of my own. I allowed someone close to me (who had no emotional ties) to dictate how I would handle the situation. I should not have done that. Now, they are both gone. All I can do is ask God to forgive me, and to ask my sister and brother-in-law to forgive me, as well.

I should have known better. Even though I have no idea how the situation would have turned out, and I can't go back in time. I have to live with this regret. I don't know how to do that, other than ask God to help me and give me peace about the situation. Of, course, I wish I had handled it differently, but it's too late. Now, all I can do is help others to really think about the decisions they have to make and hand it over to God, like I should have done, and not let outside influences dictate those decisions.

We must be very mindful of how we allow others to determine the decisions we make.

HS (Holy Spirit): *If you had a chance to go back and do over, what would you have done differently?*

ME: *I would have not left my sister alone that morning.*

HS: *What would that have required of you?*

ME: *It would have required me to communicate to someone that I wasn't comfortable with leaving her.*

HS: *How would that have gone for you?*

ME: *They would have done it.*

HS: *Why didn't you do it?*

ME: *I was being selfish, I wasn't thinking, I was in denial...I DON'T KNOW!!! (Tears flowing)*

HS: *There are decisions we must make that could mean life or death, as you have just realized.*

ME: *I know, and I made a really bad decision. I allowed pleasing someone else to override taking care of my sister.*

HS: *It's easy to replay in your mind what you should have done. Maybe there is a lesson in all this that needs to be shared with others.*

ME: *That will be the only way I can have peace about this situation. If I can help save someone else's life, but at the cost of my sister. That really hurts. I try to justify why she did what she did, but I could have prevented it from happening.*

HS: Even if you had prevented it, wouldn't it have just been prolonged? Would you have only prolonged her agony?

ME: I know without a shadow of a doubt that I would have kept her in agony with my mother. She was not going to let her go, even if I had taken her in. She would have continued to allow my mother to control her, and she would have been angry, depressed and suicidal.

HS: So, it wasn't necessarily her husband coming home that was the worst part for her?

ME: I'm not saying that. She couldn't see past him coming home. She couldn't see any way out. These were her options that we discussed with her:

- *Her husband coming home and her taking care of him, which she couldn't do anymore.*
- *Going into rehab for her opioid addition, knowing that would be like going into a psychiatric hospital, a place she had become all too familiar with and hated.*
- *Making the decision to put him in long term care, knowing that he didn't want to go there and dealing with his demands to bring him home.*

- *If he were to pass, she would be stuck with our mother manipulating and controlling her for the rest of her life.*

HS: *So, maybe you rescued her one last time?*

ME: *(silence ....)*

HS: *You always took care of her. Whenever she needed you, you were there. You had to make some tough love decisions with her. Could it be that you did what you needed to do to give her an opportunity for the only options she had left to get out of the dilemma she found herself facing?*

ME: *I had never even considered this perspective. Thank you, Lord. Maybe I didn't ask God what to do because He already knew what I needed to do. Maybe God needed me to allow this to happen as part of His plan.*

HS: *Can you honestly say that you didn't ask God? He was with you all the time. Maybe the role others played in all this was exactly what was necessary for you to fulfill God's plan?*

ME: *There are some people who have led painful lives at the cost of helping others. I'd like to believe that my sweet sister was on this earth for* *the time she was supposed to be here. I'd like to think that I can carry on her legacy by saving the lives of those who are in pain as a result of their childhood experiences.*

My biggest lesson is for people to be aware of children who experienced childhood trauma and help them.

Be there for them, be patient with them, be understanding, be nurturing.

Let them know that despite what has happened, someone loves them.

Let these adults ask God to help them.

To use them to show them how much God loves them through someone right here on earth.

Someone to let them know that they are not unworthy.

That they don't need to be thrown into a trash heap, simply because of what someone else has done.

> But in my distress, I cried out to the Lord, yes, I cried to my God for help. He heard me from his sanctuary; my cry reached his ears. (2 Samuel 22:7).

There are so many things in life that we simply do not understand. It is in those times when we must go to God for clarity. I would never have been able to move beyond my grief had I not taken it to God. God provides a perspective that is so much higher than anything we could possibly imagine. When we cry out to God, He hears us. Are you willing to hear his response?

His Timing, Not Ours

If you will recall the story of Moses (Exodus 2:11-14) and the events that transpired before he was exiled from Egypt. He was forty years old and had not yet experienced God in the way he would experience him years later. At the time, he witnessed a battle between two men: one Egyptian, one a Hebrew. Moses intervened and killed the Egyptian. He then proceeded to bury the body of the Egyptian in the sand. The next day. He ran into two Hebrew men fighting. He tried to intervene again. This time, instead of fighting, he asked a question, "Why are you fighting with your neighbor?" The man who started the altercation responded, "Who do you think you are telling us what to do?" Little did they or even Moses know the power God had placed inside of Moses. But this was not the time. This was not Moses' time. Moses' time would come in the next 40 years.

Over the next 40 years, God took Moses on quite a journey, a journey that would prepare him for what God had in store for him. Was this the plan that Moses had dreamed of? I'm sure he had dreams of one day becoming King of Egypt. He planned on marrying the King's daughter and ruling the entire kingdom. But God had other plans, plans that did not satisfy selfish desires but would change the course of the future for God's people.

Let's step back for a moment. Had Moses not killed the Egyptian, he would never have been exiled and positioned to lead the Hebrews out of Egypt and into the promised land.

What experiences have you had on your journey to fulfilling your purpose? Can you identify the key moments in your life that have allowed you to enjoy the blessings you are experiencing right now? We may see them as painful experiences, but had they not happened, we wouldn't be as far along on our journey as we are right now.

The enemy wants you to remain stuck in the moments of your painful experiences. But God wants you to understand how those painful experiences have made you who you are today. Who are you as a result? Take a moment to reflect on who you are right now and what you have been able to accomplish because of your past experiences.

When I became certified as a Life Coach 15 years ago, I realized how many of my clients were dealing with issues that stemmed from their childhood trauma. Working through my own childhood trauma, I learned the significance of setting healthy boundaries. It's difficult to set the boundaries we need to set in our lives, if we haven't dealt with our childhood trauma. Learning how and when to set healthy boundaries gives you courage to stand firm against any onset that the enemy attempts to throw along your path. Understanding your adverse childhood experiences and how they are influencing your life right now is so important. This knowledge will empower you to set the boundaries you need to regain your authentic power.

Not All Boundaries Are Created Equal

The boundaries my sisters and I experienced growing up were not healthy ones. These unhealthy boundaries were imposed upon us by someone who had not dealt with her own childhood trauma.

Much of the drama we experience as adults is the result of how we feel about ourselves. Feeling inadequate or inferior to others can cause us to set unhealthy boundaries. Learning the difference between healthy and unhealthy boundaries helps us to eliminate unnecessary drama in our lives. In order to do this, we must first come to terms with how we allowed drama to enter our lives in the first place. We may not be responsible for the drama others try to pull us into, but we are responsible for how long we allow others to pull us into their own drama.

Consequently, once I learned to identify self-defeating patterns through the process of journaling, I realized that trying to please everyone else left me empty, angry and resentful. I finally accepted the fact that I was creating my own reality. I realized I had a lot of work to do. I went to counseling. I journaled. I prayed. I realized that I could not find the answers I needed until I surrendered my life to God. These decisions led me to emotional healing. You see, we can't possibly set the boundaries we need to set until we experience emotional healing.

SUMMARY

- If we focus on our pain and disappointments, we miss out on seeing the beauty that transpires as a result.

  Take a moment to reflect on how the beauty that has transpired because of your painful past. ______________________

  ____

  ____

  ____

  ____

  ____

- The enemy wants you to remain stuck in the moments of your painful experiences, but God wants you to understand how those painful experiences have made you who you are today.

  What has God revealed to you about your purpose because of all you experienced? ______________________

  ____

  ____

  ____

  ____

  ____

  ____

- Much of the drama we experience as adults is the result of how we feel about ourselves.

  What connection have you made between your past experiences and your current challenges? ____________

- We can't possibly set the boundaries we need to set until we experience emotional healing.

  How important is it to you, to heal from your painful past? What will change for you? ____________

CHAPTER 4

CAUTION – ROADBLOCKS AHEAD

Nothing is more frustrating than moving forward only to encounter roadblocks along the way.

My husband and I take road trips quite often. For each trip, we plan our itinerary very carefully. Over the years, we have learned to allow time in our schedule for situations that may occur which are beyond our control.

When we travel by car, we often run into either road construction, auto accidents or even roadblocks. Each of these uncontrolled circumstances would cause quite a glitch in our plans, if we didn't allow time for them. When we learn to anticipate them, we don't get overly frustrated.

My goal is to help you get where you're going in life, while anticipating roadblocks. Our roadblocks are often a result of our adverse childhood experiences. These roadblocks can appear quite quickly and unexpectedly. If we don't anticipate them, they can cause a disruption that could make us want to turn around and give up altogether.

Occasionally, we unconsciously react to people, events or circumstances based on emotions that surface because of childhood trauma. Learning how to become more conscious of our reactions helps us to increase our level of self-awareness. Once we know better, we do better, thereby reducing the amount of frustration and drama in our lives.

In his book The Slight Edge,[5] Jeff Olson offers suggestions on how one small adjustment in our actions can yield better results. When we encounter situations that trigger painful emotions, a slight shift in the way we process the situation can be very helpful. This small adjustment in the way we process the experience can help us to yield results that benefit us.

Oftentimes, the emotions we act upon are influenced by past experiences. These painful experiences, whether we realize it or not, are guiding our decisions like a rudder on a ship. A rudder that is calibrated based on a faulty map can only lead to disaster. When our past hurts are used as the map we follow and we use this to determine our response to a given situation, we will most likely veer off course from our intended destination.

Let me give you an example. When someone points out a mistake I have made, my immediate response is anger. I perceive their comments as "attacks on my character", and I get defensive. As I step back to consider the origin of my emotions, I realize that the reason for my anger in these situations goes back to something that happened to me when I was fifteen years old.

My mother had scheduled a modeling call for me. She had arranged a cab to pick me up and take me to the location. This was the first time I had taken a cab, let alone by myself.

At the time, I never understood why passengers sat in the backseat of a cab. I thought it was quite an unfriendly gesture. In my mind, the people who rode in the back seat of a car thought they were better than the person who was courteous enough to drive them to where they wanted to go. Keep in mind, I was only fifteen years old at the time.

When the cab arrived to pick me up, I asked the driver if I could sit in the front seat. He hesitated for a moment then replied, "Sure." And moved his items off the passenger seat so I could sit.

When I arrived at my destination, my mother was standing in the parking lot waiting to pay the cab fare. Before I could get out of the taxicab, she began to yell at me for sitting in the front seat. She enlisted all sorts of curse words and accusations on my character for the decision I made to sit in the front seat. I was sure that her voice could be heard a mile away. I was thoroughly embarrassed and felt like a complete idiot.

From that point on, I began to question every decision I made:

Would it be the right decision?

Would it be a stupid decision?

Would I be embarrassed?

Would I be the laughingstock?

When I stepped back to assess my anger, I realized why I tended to react this way. Gaining this new awareness helped me to identify why I react the way I do. This new awareness allows me to consider what is being said, who's saying it, and why rather than considering it a personal attack on my character.

Let's face it, people are hurting. Their pain is causing them to take actions and make decisions based on that hurt, sometimes without even realizing it. When we take the time to consider the origin of our pain, we free ourselves to examine reasons for our discontent. Believe me, it's not always someone else at fault. Sometimes, it's our very own self-sabotaging beliefs.

If your life seems chaotic, full of drama, confusion, frustration and disappointment, then it's time to get to the core of your chaos. What is it that's causing this chaos? Could it be that your past trauma has influenced where you are right now?

Let's learn more about how your adverse childhood experiences may be affecting your current reality and preventing you from re-claiming your authentic power.

SUMMARY

• When you encounter situations that trigger painful emotions, a slight shift in the way you process the situation can be very helpful. This small adjustment can help you to yield results that benefit you rather than cause you more pain and frustration.

What situation(s) have you experienced that triggered painful emotions? ________________________________

____

____

____

____

• Learning how to become more conscious of your reactions helps to increase your level of self-awareness. Once you know better, you do better, thereby reducing the amount of frustration and drama in your life.

How can you move from reacting to responding in the situation(s) you indicated above? ____________________

____

____

____

____

____

- When you take the time to consider the origin of your pain, you free yourself to examine the reason for your discontent.

  How are you allowing your painful past to affect your level of discontent? ______________________________

  ____
  ____
  ____
  ____
  ____
  ____
  ____

- If your life seems chaotic, full of drama, confusion, frustration and disappointment, then it's time to get to the core of your chaos. What is it that's causing this chaos? Could it be that your past trauma has influenced where you are right now?

  What is it that is causing your chaos? ______________

  ____
  ____
  ____
  ____
  ____
  ____
  ____
  ____
  ____

CHAPTER 5

SELF-DISCOVERY

"There is a very human tendency to deny the fallacies and tragedies in our lives, but these are the very things that sometimes deliver us to ourselves – if we can learn from them."

Jane Fonda, Prime Time[6]

By now, you have a better understanding of your painful childhood experiences. Have you considered how your experiences are impacting your life today? How do these experiences influence your decision making and how have these experiences shaped your relationships?

You may be at a place where you believe you have overcome these painful experiences, so they don't affect you or anyone else around you.

You've done the work, and you are at peace.

You have forgiven those who have inflicted pain on you and are ready to put all that behind you.

You believe it's better to let the past stay in the past and move forward.

On the other hand, you may not have forgiven the individuals who have caused you pain, but you don't believe that has any bearing on where you are in life. Maybe the pain that was inflicted upon you was so bad that you have avoided dealing with it altogether.

Trust me, I have been in each of these positions at one point or another.

No matter our decision, life goes on until it doesn't. We grow up and live our lives the way we think we should. We go to school, we pursue a career, we start a business, we join churches, groups or organizations, we get married, we start families, we grow older, we retire, then we die. Not necessarily in that order, we live our lives in between what's called, "the dash". That time between our birth and our death.

Trying to come into our own through the pain of a childhood fraught with parental abandonment, addictions, and exposure to situations far too complex for our delicate minds to understand can leave us in a state of delusion as to the realities of life.

As we enter the realm of adulthood and begin to travel on our chosen roads toward the life we expect, the past can creep up on us like an unexpected bacterial cyst, a re-occurring outbreak when it's least expected. Our daydreams and temporary fantasies of a childhood filled with Brady Bunch love and Walton Family values provided us with a momentary haven amid our chaotic world, only to awaken us by the abrupt reality of a family competing with the likes of The Adams Family and The Simpsons.

Reflections

My Journal Entry

I listened to a couple of tapes as well as reading one of my sister's journals. It was important to discover that the reason she didn't stop talking to our mother is because she was afraid of her. The fear that our mother instilled in her was paralyzing.

Even my sister's journal entries conveyed the fear she had for her. At one point, she wrote big on two pieces of paper, "Lord, I'm done with being here. Tell our older sister [who passed] I'm coming. Tell Mother, 'Thanks a lot'." She wrote," if this is what love is then I don't want to be here." I believe this was one of the times when she attempted suicide.

My twin sister's suicidal thoughts began in 1999. She endured for another 22 years as she struggled with depression, feeling unloved and unable to trust God. Even though she loved the Lord, she beat herself up for not trusting Him.

She shared several traumatic childhood events with her therapist to discover how he would have handled the situation as a loving parent. She was always looking to prove that she had the worst childhood. She was fixated on finding out how other people grew up, learning what their childhood was like growing up. It seemed to prove to her that she was justified in feeling as bad as she did and for struggling as much as she did with her childhood experiences. She sought after parents who would share how they raised their children and would ask each of them how they would handle a particular situation that she experienced.

I was thinking about this situation driving home yesterday, and I thought about how much I tried to help her. I tried to coach her. She wasn't coachable. She didn't want to get out of her situation. She wanted others to change, not her. If she had only distanced herself from the people who were reminding her of her past. That would have taken courage, courage she didn't have. It was safer for her to stay miserable in her situation than to consider other possibilities. Every time she called me, I offered possible solutions. She didn't want to act on these solutions. She simply wanted to tell me how miserable she was. As a matter of fact, she would call her friend instead of me. She wanted to remain a victim. She knew that I wouldn't allow her to embrace the victim role. She was very concerned about people being mad at her.

The fear that our mother instilled in my sister was unbelievable, so much fear that she couldn't take the fact that she would still have to deal with our mother even after her husband passed away. Even though I was willing to help her, and she knew I would, she could not rid herself of our mother out of fear.

It's interesting to me how she would find every opportunity to prove that our mother was a bad parent, yet she continued to have her as a part of her life out of fear. That had to be such a horrible existence.

It takes courage to consider suicide, but it takes fear to give you the courage to carry it out.

So, she took her life to escape having to deal with our mother. Wow...that is so very sad on so many levels. That means that there was nothing I could have done to prevent her from taking her life.

If your childhood was less than that Brady Bunch life you imagined, the enemy will try to convince you that you aren't smart enough, or pretty enough, or strong enough to go after the life you really want. These debilitating thoughts he plants in your mind will show up in the form of doubt, fear, insecurities, and hopelessness.

It's time to examine these self-defeating beliefs. That's the only way to overcome them. Your past was not meant to hinder you but to serve as the backdrop for your future success. The first step in eliminating the enemy's lies is to address them, to face them head on.

I want you to take a moment to consider your "dash". What would you like to accomplish in your lifetime? What do you dream about? What would you do if nothing was stopping you? As you consider your answers to these questions, keep in mind that whatever it is you want to do, the ability is already inside of you. Unfortunately, that ability is better known by the enemy than you. Because the enemy knows what you are capable of, he will use every obstacle he can to prevent you from pursuing your dreams.

The Underdog Fallacy

We tend to think of the underdog as someone who is not expected to win, someone who is a victim to their circumstances. We tend to root for the underdogs because we think they are at a "disadvantage". Let's face it, everyone loves a victory story, especially when the odds are stacked against the winner. We can consider ourselves the underdogs in many situations where our memories of our past make us feel unable to succeed in areas where we would like. But let's take a closer look at a perfect example of a false belief as it relates to being considered an "underdog."

You have no doubt heard the biblical account of David and Goliath in the Book of Samuel. In this story, David, carrying only stones and a slingshot, is considered the underdog who slays the giant. Here was David, a kid and a shepherd boy, going up against a giant, an experienced warrior. We know that Goliath stood almost 7 feet tall, and that David was small in stature, somewhere between 4'11 and 5'0 tall. As they each prepared for battle, Goliath wore a heavy suit of armor and carried a sword and a javelin as weapons. All David had was a sling.

Was David really the underdog in this scenario? While it may seem that David was no match for the giant Goliath, he had quite an advantage, just not the advantage one would presume through the naked eye.

As a shepherd tending to his father's flock of sheep, David was responsible for protecting the herd. David's responsibilities as a shepherd brought him face to face with animals that threatened to kill his flock of sheep. Because of this, he learned to use a sling and rocks to ward off any threats against his flock. He proficiently used his sling as a weapon to kill a bear and a lion.

To assume that David was at a disadvantage in his battle against Goliath is incorrect. You see, in ancient times, there were three types of warriors: cavalry, heavy infantry and artillery. Cavalry soldiers rode on horseback or in chariots. Heavy infantry soldiers were considered foot soldiers and trained for close battle with heavy weapons and armor. The artillery soldiers were trained to use slings. This is not your childhood slingshot that most writers refer to when they mention David and his slingshot. This sling was an incredibly devastating weapon. Consider David's stones. They were not your normal rocks. These stones were barium sulfate, which was twice the density of normal stones.[6] Artillery soldiers were incredibly accurate with their slings. They were trained to be very precise when aiming at their target.

While David was not trained as a soldier, he taught himself how to use a sling to protect his father's flock of sheep. Without even realizing it, David had been equipped to fight his most important battle. What skills have you developed over the years that will prove to be useful in your future battles?

By the time I graduated high school, I had attended 13 different schools. This made it extremely difficult to build and maintain friendships. At the age of 12, I was given a diary for my birthday. My key-laden diary became my only reliable confidante, my constant companion. Her name was first Kit-Kat, then Kitty, a new nickname for each new diary begun. Her identity was changed for her, as it was for me with each new transfer. It was no different from the constant change I had become accustomed to. My diary and I shared many experiences. We laughed and cried together continuously as the years passed by.

Writing in my diary and in later years my journals has unveiled a valuable tool for moving me through life's terrain. It has given me the ability to examine my experiences and develop a plan of action for identifying any historical data that may be hindering my forward movement toward the life that God has pre-destined for me. The practice of journaling has equipped me to write. Little did I know at the age of 12 that God was equipping me to help others through my practice of journaling. What I have come to realize is that the practice of journaling is one of the deadliest weapons we can use against the enemy, because it allows us to transition our emotions into constructive thought, thus moving us toward solutions. This practice of journaling has equipped me to share these lessons with you.

The Adversary

Now that you have a better understanding of David and his expertise with a sling, let's take a closer look at Goliath. This heavy infantry soldier fully expected that his challenge for a 1 on 1 battle would place him face to face with an infantry soldier. But what happened when he was faced with an opponent who had skills different from his? As we consider Goliath's strengths, his ability to intimidate based on his stature, let's consider his weaknesses. Bible scholars believe that Goliath was led onto the valley floor by a man carrying his shield. Why would a soldier of this stature need someone to stand in front of him?

According to Malcolm Gladwell's research[7], there has been a lot of speculation about Goliath's height. These speculations have concluded that Goliath had a form of giantism called acromegaly. Acromegaly is caused by a benign tumor on the pituitary gland that causes an overproduction of human growth hormones. One of the side effects of acromegaly is vison abnormalities. Goliath commands David to "come to him". He must ask him to come to him because Goliath couldn't see him clearly. Because of Goliath's condition, what we consider as Goliath's greatest strength, his height, is his greatest weakness.

As you can see, David was not the underdog, after all, and neither are you. Consider your own experiences. How have they equipped you to fight your most important battles? Everything you have gone through has made you who you are today. All your experiences have been aligned to prepare you for your future battles as well as your future victories.

> “The wise man conquers the strong man and levels his defenses.” (Proverbs 20:22 the Living Bible)

When you consider your adversary, consider his weaknesses. Things are not always as they appear. The enemy wants nothing more than to keep you in bondage to your past hurts. Gaining self-awareness helps you to discover your gifts, your talents and your strengths, all the things that the enemy doesn’t want you to discover. Grab your weapons, and let’s go after the life God has prepared us to conquer!

SUMMARY

- Your past was not meant to hinder you but to serve as the backdrop for your future success.

  How can you use your painful past to create your future success? ____

  ____

  ____

  ____

  ____

  ____

  ____

  ____

- Whatever it is you want to do, the ability is already inside of you.

  What will it take from you to create that success? __________

  ____

  ____

  ____

  ____

  ____

  ____

  ____

  ____

• The practice of journaling is one of the deadliest weapons you can use against the enemy, because it allows you to transition your emotions into constructive thought and move you toward solutions.

How have your answers to these journal prompts helped you so far? ____

____

____

____

____

____

____

____

____

• When you consider your adversary, consider his weaknesses. Things are not always as they appear. The enemy wants nothing more than to keep you in bondage to your past hurts.

How is the enemy using your weakness to keep you from moving forward? ____

____

____

____

____

____

____

How can his weakness give you an advantage? __________

____

____

____

____

____

- Gaining self-awareness helps you to discover your gifts, your talents and your strengths, all the things that the enemy doesn't want you to discover.

  What gifts and talents have you uncovered through the work you have done so far in this book? __________________

____

____

____

____

____

____

____

____

____

____

____

____

____

____

____

____

CHAPTER 6

BEHAVIORAL PATTERNS

"We are blessed, every one of us, with gifts that are needed by others who are traveling this path with us, but until we are free to see who we really are, we will not be able to recognize that which we have been created to give, and until we can care deeply for others from a more objective perspective, we will not be able to give our special gifts to the world around us."

Karen Casey, "Let Go Now"

What is A Pattern?

A pattern is defined as a regular or repeated way in which something happens or is done (Collins English Dictionary). A pattern is something that flows a particular way. It has a consistent flow. A pattern is also something we follow. There are patterns that inspire us to create and those that we want to duplicate.

If you know anything about design, you know that it begins with a pattern. I create beautiful crochet pieces that start with a pattern. If I don't follow the pattern correctly, my project will not come out correctly, and that's a lot of wasted time and effort.

There are patterns we create in our lives, patterns we follow, whether consciously or unconsciously; some are healthy, while some are not so healthy. We don't often realize when the patterns we follow are detrimental to living the life we would like to, where we achieve great successes, where we have peace in any given area, or where we set proper boundaries, both internal and external.

I want to help you identify behavioral patterns in your life, patterns of behavior that are mere remnants from your past, behaviors that manifest quite frequently and unconsciously. These self-defeating patterns of behavior cause us to repeat the same mistakes and yield undesired results. It's not until we are willing to identify these self-defeating patterns that we can eliminate them.

The patterns that shape our lives can be identified through our willingness to journal. Yes, writing in a journal and going back over what we have written over time. Our commitment to this practice can make the difference between living a life of frustration and one of complete peace and joy!

You must understand that writing is something that doesn't come easy to most people. Life events are much more important. The immediate reactions to these life events are much more prevalent than taking the time to stop and think as a prerequisite to acting or responding. You see, the heart lends little time to reason. That's the head's job. Allowing the heart to rule over the head makes for disastrous results. Journaling requires the head (brain) to take precedence over the heart.

The practice of journaling allows you to see something for what it truly is and to draw conclusions based on those findings. Your decisions at that point are based on a concerted effort between your head and your heart.

There comes a time in our lives (and that time may be right now for you) when we realize that something needs to change. Unfortunately, expecting someone else to change is not always the solution. Many times, we must do the changing. We can do this by identifying patterns that are keeping us from moving closer to where we want to be.

C.A.R.I.N.G.

I want to help you identify those self-defeating patterns by sharing a formula I created to gain control over these patterns. This formula will take you from unconsciousness to awareness of the behavioral patterns that prevent you from moving forward. The use of journaling with this formula allows you to see something for what it truly is and draw conclusions based on what you discover about a situation, about a person, or, most importantly, about yourself.

C - CAPTURE YOUR WORDS

Get it out of your head and your heart and down on paper. This is best achieved by using a style of journaling referred to as cathartic. Cathartic is a way to purge and cleanse. When you write in your journal, get it all out on paper. I typically refer to this as spewing. The more we can get out on paper, the less destruction it can cause in our heads. Believe it or not, you already practice cathartic journaling any time you share your thoughts or opinions about a particular topic through social media, whether through your own post or in response to someone else's, or if you send a text to someone and it's filled with emotions. These are both forms of cathartic journaling.

A - ACKNOWLEDGE

This is when you re-read what you have written and allow your head to speak to your heart.

R - REVISIT

This is when you reflect on your past journal entries and begin to identify any patterns of behavior, outcomes or reactions. NOTE: Reactions are a response to an emotion.

I - INVESTIGATE

In order to respond appropriately, you want to step back long enough to investigate the reason for your reaction to a given situation by getting to the true source of the problem. There are several journaling styles that can help you to uncover the reason for your particular reaction; Dialogical and Proprioceptive. These two advanced journaling styles help you to expose details that don't readily come to mind. They offer an open window into the origin of your discontent, thereby increasing your level of self-awareness.

N - NAME THE SOURCE

This is where you begin to identify the source. You take the time to consider your answers to the following questions:

What have I learned about this situation or about myself?

What pattern do I see?

Why is this a pattern?

Why am I allowing this in my life?

What can I do about it?

You may not identify a pattern through a single journal entry. It will take going back through several past journal entries and incorporating a form of journaling called "lists". Going through past journal entries will help you to capture repeat patterns onto a list you create that will illuminate patterns for you.

G – GENERATE POWER

Once you've done the work of answering the questions above, you now have the power to accept your responsibility and the power to change. Now that you know better, you do better. You have the power to change. It's all on you.

Once you commit to using this formula, you gain clarity about your self-defeating patterns. Now you can do something about them. You now have the power to set healthy boundaries, both internally and externally. Your internal boundaries dictate what you will and won't tolerate; your external boundaries allow you to communicate your boundaries to others. It is very difficult to communicate your external boundaries if you haven't established your internal boundaries. This becomes much easier when you make a commitment to taking what you have learned through this journaling exercise and decide that you're not going to accept this behavior any longer and begin to dissolve the self-defeating pattern that allowed this behavior to dominate your reactions.

The goal in using this formula is to increase your level of self-awareness. How you use the information you uncover is totally up to you. My desire is for you to gain a better understanding of your own patterns. The more you understand them, the more empowered you become to change them. If what you uncover is painful, stand firm. Allow that pain to change you so you can thrive.

Now that you have the formula to increase your level of self-awareness, let's look at a few behavioral patterns that are common for those who have experienced some form of childhood trauma.

SUMMARY

- It's not until we are willing to identify our self-defeating patterns that we can eliminate them.

- The patterns that shape our lives can be identified through our willingness to journal. Your commitment to this practice can make the difference between living a life of frustration and one of complete peace and joy!

- The practice of journaling allows you to see something for what it truly is and to draw conclusions based on those findings. Your decisions at that point are based on a concerted effort between your head and your heart.

What self-defeating patterns have you identified through your reading, reflection, and journal prompt responses?

___

___

___

___

___

___

___

- C.A.R.I.N.G. – A formula that will take you from unconsciousness to awareness of the behavioral patterns that prevent you from moving forward.

- The more you understand your own self-defeating patterns, the more empowered you become to change them.

Using this C.A.R.I.N.G. formula, how have you increased your level of self-awareness?

C - CAPTURE YOUR WORDS ____________________

____

A - ACKNOWLEDGE ____________________________

____

R - REVISIT ________________________________

____

I - INVESTIGATE _____________________________

____

N - NAME THE SOURCE ________________________

____

G – GENERATE POWER ________________________

____

CHAPTER 7
CODEPENDENCY

CODEPENDENT – WHO ME?

The first emotion I can remember feeling was empathy. I'm sure I experienced other feelings, but this one stands out. I was a very protective of my mother as a child. In fact, it was an obsession. I tried very hard to soothe her when she was sad. She would cry over something, and I felt so bad for her. I didn't want to see her sad or hurting. Unfortunately, I don't recall her ever soothing me when I was sad or hurting. But then again, I don't think I ever revealed those feelings to her. Maybe I never had those feelings. I discovered at a very early age that my mother could care less than a damn about my feelings, so why show them?

I knew my mother wasn't happy in life, and it was important for me to make her happy. It was important to be with her because I wanted her attention. I wanted her love. I came to resent her for wanting special attention from me. She wanted me to soothe

> her. If she had a husband, I wouldn't have had to soothe her, her husband would have that role. I hated having to rub her back all the time. I HATED IT!
>
> Journal Entry, My Twin

Codependency is one of those buzz words that has received a lot of attention in the past few years. I began reading up on codependency when I realized that my emotions were based on the emotions of those around me. Growing up in a dysfunctional environment, my sisters and I never knew what to expect when our mother came home. The tone would be set for us once she walked in the door. We could judge her mood based on her facial expression. When a child sees a parent walking through the door, it's usually a joyous occasion. We envisioned us all running into her arms and receiving a group hug, knowing that she was happy to see us. But in our home, it was a different story.

Whenever we heard her car pull into the driveway or heard the door open, we would practically hold our breath in fear. We would wait until we saw her face to interpret her emotional disposition. Her temperament would determine the atmosphere in our home for the rest of the day. We were quite proficient at reading her facial expressions. If she came home in a bad mood, my older sister would continue doing what she was doing, my twin sister would try everything she could to get my mother into a better mood, and I would retreat into my room, looking for a way to distance myself from the possible rage that was likely to come next.

One of the consequences of adverse childhood experiences that my sisters and I shared was becoming people pleasers. We were afraid to dis-please others for fear of what would happen to us. Growing up in our household, we didn't share our opinions on anything around our mother for fear of how she would respond. Her anger was the kind that injured us, through either verbal attacks, physical beatings, or threat of taking something away that we loved dearly. This often involved forbidding us from communicating with the people we loved the most. We would even hold our breath when she had an altercation with someone else for fear of how we would be affected by it.

My mother hated when my grandmother would come upstairs. In my mother's word's, she only came upstairs to our home to be nosy and get into her business. My mother hated it when my grandmother complained about something my mother was doing or not doing. Every time they had an argument, we weren't allowed to talk to my grandparents who lived downstairs from us. I wasn't allowed to go downstairs and eat dinner with them anymore, even when there was no food in our house. It hurt my grandmother so much when we refused to talk to her whenever we saw her. I saw it on her face. There were many times when we were forbidden to have anything to do with my grandparents. That hurt me probably as much as it hurt my grandmother. I obeyed my mother and ignored my grandmother whenever I saw her because if I didn't I would either get slapped in the face or get a whooping and I didn't want to piss her off. I wanted to stay on her good side.

Journal Entry, My Twin

Growing into adulthood, I allowed other people to dictate how I lived my life because I feared what would happen when I said no. Growing up, my "no" was followed by either a back handed slap in the face or ridicule that only increased the more time passed.

What is Codependency?

In the simplest terms, codependency refers to a persistent pattern of behavior that includes suppressing your own needs to meet the needs of others. The term "codependency" was once reserved for partners of those living with a substance use disorder, but the definition has since expanded to include all kinds of relationships.

Codependency is not a formal diagnosis in the Diagnostic and Statistical Manual of Mental Disorders, 5th ed. (DSM-5). Instead, it's more of a group of traits and a relational style. It is most common in families with mental health conditions, medical disability, or with those who have experienced generational trauma.

"It is when compassion turns to a compulsion to care for others," says Mary Joye, a licensed mental health counselor in Winter Haven, Florida. "It feels as if you are living someone else's life for them. You give up your own desires and needs to keep others happy."[8]

If you consider yourself a people pleaser, this does not mean you are codependent. A kind and giving heart can increase the levels of oxytocin (a hormone that encourages relaxation and lowers anxiety) and dopamine (the chemical that mediates pleasure) in our brains. It makes us feel good to help others. On the other hand, if you are codependent, you tend to want to please others at the expense of your own happiness.

My sister was codependent. There was something inside of her that caused her to please others at the expense of her happiness and well-being. She shared a lot of her people pleasing frustrations with me, especially the times she put our mother's needs and her husband's needs ahead of her own.

There is usually a significant amount of fear when making the decision to please others above what's best for you. It feels like you, alone, are solely responsible for another person's well-being. When people know that you are a people pleaser, they will manipulate you to do things that are best for them with no consideration for what's best for you. My sister lost her sense of self. As a result, she fell deeper and deeper into depression and feelings of worthlessness. I witnessed her needs, taking a backseat to the demands placed on her by both her husband and our mother.

Codependency is like alcoholism in that it doesn't go away. It's always there, but you can recover. It's an ongoing process.

I am codependent. One of the by-products of growing up in a dysfunctional single parent home with an abusive, alcohol and drug addicted mother is co-dependency. Working through my own issues because of this has been painful work but not as painful as staying in that cycle of dysfunction. I believe the reason I can establish healthy boundaries in my life is because I accept the reality of codependency. Understanding how I tend to please others helps me to step back and assess how I am feeling about pleasing others. It also allows me the time I need to identify patterns of behavior, not only in myself but in others who try to take advantage of my desire to please.

When we fall into the realm of taking on the responsibility of others who are fully capable of taking on the responsibility for themselves, we maintain our codependency and end up suffering more in the end.

"Since codependence is the result of dysfunctional parenting that abuses the normal characteristics of children by harmful actions or by neglect, recovery involves reviewing your past to identify formative experiences in your early life that were less-than-nurturing or traumatic. (Pia Mellody, "Facing Codependence")[9]

Codependence involves so much more than people-pleasing. Pia Mellody has taken a bold step by creating an extensive guide that reflects the research and clinical work at The Meadows Treatment Center. She provides a comprehensive framework that will help you to understand codependency and the role it plays in our lives as adults. Her book Facing Codependence has helped me to gain insight into how different predicaments I found myself in were influenced by my painful childhood experiences.

SUMMARY

- Codependency refers to a persistent pattern of behavior that includes suppressing your own needs to meet the needs of others.

  *We all do this at one time or another. Identify a time when you suppressed your needs for others. What was your reason for meeting their needs instead of yours?*_____________

  ____

  ____

  ____

- If you are codependent, you tend to want to please others at the expense of your own happiness.

  *How often do you find yourself pleasing others at the expense of your own happiness?*___________________________

  ____

  ____

  What has that cost you? __________________________

  ____

  ____

  How do you feel about that? _______________________

  ____

  ____

  ____

What can you do about that? ______________________

____

____

What are you WILLING to do about that? ____________

____

____

- When people know that you are a people pleaser, they will manipulate you to do things that are best for them with no consideration for what's best for you.

Who are the people in your life that do this? __________

____

____

____

____

____

- When you fall into the realm of taking on the responsibility of others who are fully capable of taking on the responsibility for themselves, you maintain your codependency and end up suffering more in the end.

How does this statement resonate with you? __________

____

____

____

____

CHAPTER 8

EMOTIONAL TRIGGERS

Therapeutic Notes on my Twin:

> Patient found employment during the mid-1980's as a caseworker with Children and Youth Services, a state agency for preventing and investigating child abuse. She reports that she was respected for her work. While employed with Children and Youth Services, she attended an in-service training for detecting and intervening with children who were being sexually abused. During the training, she experienced a panic attack and left the room. Subsequently, she found that she could not stay focused on her work and resigned this position.

When we think of situations that cause us to react emotionally, it's important that we identify our triggers:

WHAT ARE TRIGGERS?

Triggers are those painful experiences from our past that have grown scars. Whenever we experience anything that closely resembles that pain, our scars begin to expose the wounds and we begin to react to this all too familiar experience in a way that attempts to protect the wound from further pain.

Many people try to ignore their past traumas. It's in the past, let's keep it there, right? If we don't talk about it, it will go away, like dust swept under a rug. The problem is that as we grow into adulthood, those dust bunnies that were swept under the rug have a way of re-appearing and wreaking havoc in our lives.

These dust bunnies are our triggers. When we face adversities as we all do, our dust bunnies surface. When that rug we used to hide the dust (our painful experiences) is pulled up, each particle is exposed for all to see. Sadly, if we don't stop long enough to discern each pile of dirt (the trauma from our past), we fail to understand how these experiences are influencing our current reality.

But who has time? We have adult responsibilities: school to attend, a job to go to, a relationship to secure, a career to pursue, and/or children to care for. All of these pursuits become derailed at one point or another when we fail to address our childhood trauma.

We must make the time to understand how our painful unwarranted experiences are affecting us in our daily lives. Could our past experiences have something to do with the decisions we are making and the positions we find ourselves in today? Far too often, it's how we process our experiences that prevents us from living the life we imagined.

Recording Insights:

My sister and her therapist discussed how her anxiety and depression were triggered through her work as a caseworker at a Children and Youth agency. Having parents repeatedly ridicule her, yell at her, issue death threats and spew accusations toward her caused her own experiences of child abuse to surface.

We are currently witnessing history in the making with this year's Olympic games in Tokyo. America's sweetheart, Simone Biles, decided to back out of gymnastics competition after experiencing a setback. There were many speculations as to why she chose not to compete. During one of her television interviews in Tokyo, she stated that she experienced a "trigger". Something happened during her time in Tokyo that triggered an emotional response. This emotional response gave her an opportunity to step back and assess her current mental and physical state.

Our triggers are our pre-conditioned beliefs about ourselves based on the painful experiences we have had in our past that surface when we feel victimized in one way or another. Our natural response in these uncomfortable situations is based on these triggers. Our negative experiences create filters as a form of protection. These filters act as barriers to protect us from the impact of the bad experiences that caused us so much pain.

When you think of a filter in a coffee pot, the role of the filter is to allow the water to flow through without the coffee grounds flowing into the coffee. It is a safety net. This filter allows us the opportunity to enjoy the coffee. Just like the filter is used to keep the coffee grounds out, our filters are a way for us to separate the bad and preserve what is good. We pull these triggers when we believe that a filter is not in place to protect us from the harm that others inflict on us; be it mental, emotional, or physical.

We may never know what trigger Simone Biles experienced; it's really none of our business. But the fact that she identified her trigger and responded in a way that protected her mental health was quite commendable. She used a filter to manage the trigger that impacted her mental and physical health. She chose not to compete. This was a healthy response to a situation that could have been devastating had she allowed it to spiral out of control. Some might say she forfeited her chance to "win the gold". Her dedication to her profession was not in question. Her commitment to her mental health was her priority. Sometimes, we must do what's best for us rather than what is expected of us. We must live with the outcome of the decisions we make. I know her decision took a lot of courage, and I am extremely proud of her for putting her mental and physical health above the needs of everyone else. Her role as a gymnast may just be the beginning that set the stage for her lifetime legacy.

God's Plan is Much Bigger

> Trust in the Lord with all thine heart and lean not to thine own understanding. In all thy ways acknowledge Him and He shall direct your path (Proverbs 3:5 KJV)

We must remember that our God-given purpose is ALWAYS to impact the lives of others. The route He chooses for us to carry this out is usually a mystery. No matter where we find ourselves through the gifts and talents that God has given us, it is so important that we use them for His glory and not our own.

We don't always understand why we are on the path we find ourselves walking. We can't anticipate the detours. All we can do is trust God to lead us on the path towards His chosen destination for us. We may experience disappointments along the way. We may blame our current reality on our past traumas.

It's easier to blame than to claim.

It's easier to place blame on our past than it is to claim victory over our future. What if we trusted God? What if we knew that all our experiences were preparing us for His use and His glory? What if we trusted His plan instead of our own? Could it be that our past experiences are the foundation for our future victories?

Our triggers are our pre-conditioned beliefs about ourselves based on the painful experiences we have had in our past that surface when we feel victimized in one way or another. Our natural response in these uncomfortable situations is based on these triggers.

Our triggers are carnal. Our filters are a choice. We can choose to filter our experiences through God's Word and through prayer, or we can choose an unhealthy filter. An unhealthy response is attributed to our learned behavior, the way we immediately react to a given situation.

Let me give you an example.

IMPATIENCE

You find yourself growing impatient with someone. Ask yourself:

- What about this situation is causing me to be impatient?
- Which experiences have I had that make me impatient in this situation?

In this example, you allow yourself to step back to consider the what vs. the who. It may not be the person, even though the person is the one you react to. But thinking through the WHAT will allow you to respond quite differently. This will allow you to control the emotion vs. the emotion controlling you, thereby eliminating the possibility of damaging a relationship.

This is how we guard our hearts with all diligence or guard our "temperament" with all "attentiveness" – by paying attention to the situations that trigger our knee-jerk reactions. Our increased awareness helps us to respond in a more productive manner.

Oftentimes, without even realizing it, we react through emotions, but we respond through thought and consideration. As you take the time to consider your answers to these questions, you gain a better understanding of yourself. You've taken the time to identify the "trigger", and you've let the other person know that you value them based on your response vs. your reaction.

The C.O.R.E. Model

Are you aware of your triggers?

Many of the conflicts we find ourselves involved in are based on our triggers. Let's look at a few triggers. Are any of these familiar to you?

Impatience (we've discussed in the example)

Lack of trust

Resistance to change

Relationship tension

Filters/History

Negativity

A spirit of offense

Self-preservation

In his bestselling book The Purpose Driven Life, Rick Warren[10] states that "often the way we handle a conflict creates a bigger hurt than the original problem itself." When we take the time to consider our own part in a conflict by identifying the triggers that may be playing a part in our reaction, we are open to hearing a perspective different from our own. This consideration places us in a better position to set the boundaries needed to create collaboration vs. dissention.

When we experience any of these situations, we automatically refer to the memory of a previous situation. It's a knee-jerk reaction. Any of these triggers can cause us to "lock and load", meaning we prepare ourselves for battle. We are ready to react to others in a way that may not be the best way to resolve an issue. These situations are our triggers. Instead of reacting to a given situation based on our trigger, it's important that we step back long enough to assess how to respond in a healthy way.

There were times when we weren't allowed to defend ourselves. As adults, we now have an opportunity to defend ourselves but in a way that doesn't jeopardize our emotions, our livelihood or even our peace of mind.

To help you gain a larger perspective on a given situation before any damage is done, let's consider ***C.O.R.E.*** This model has helped me many times to respond appropriately when I experience a situation that triggers the memory of a previous painful experience.

C - Consider Origins:

What Is My Reality? What Is Their Reality?

Take time to step back and consider your reality and the origin of the person you are in conflict with. What is the reality for the other person (realizing that the two realities are very different)?

- Could it be that they [or you] are reacting or responding based on their [or your] own filters, i.e., family dynamics; their childhood achievements were never good enough, so they feel they need to prove themselves and are always seeking approval?
- Could it be that they [or you] had controlling, domineering parents, so they don't set appropriate boundaries with their superiors, yet they treat employees like children?
- What is the trigger at play here?
- Is it appropriate to react to this person or situation based on my trigger?
- If so, why?
- Which issue am I addressing and what outcome am I looking for?

These are a lot of questions to answer. You may not need to answer all of them, based on the situation, but considering your answers to each of these questions will help you to determine your best response.

O – Own the Outcome

Take responsibility for your role in each situation. Not only in the dilemma but also in the result realizing that you have control over your response but no one else's.

This isn't easy, but it's important to remember that the way we handle a conflict can create a bigger hurt than the original problem itself.

Ask God to give you a better understanding of the situation so that your response is a healthy one. Remember my journal entry I shared with you in Chapter 3 where I shared an example of Dialogical journaling? You can also use this style of journaling to help you. Working through a script lets you have a conversation with someone in your journal and sheds light on different perspectives. It can even give you a better understanding of the person you are at odds with.

R – Remember Your "WHY"

What are you looking to achieve? So many times, the enemy uses conflict to serve as a distraction from completing the work at hand. His interference can cause us to either retreat or attack. Either reaction takes us off course. This is a sure way to prevent you from moving forward.

Take some time to journal the purpose and the goal with the person or people you are in conflict with. In other words, attack the problem, not the person. The enemy uses people to stop us in our tracks. When we can identify the problem, we are in a better position to solve it and move forward without allowing the enemy to control us through our emotions.

E – Eliminate Unhealthy Filters

Identify the triggers that surface as a result of the "baggage" or painful experiences that may be preventing you from being objective so that you can focus on reconciliation. The problem will then lose its significance and place you in a much better position to collaborate in the future.

Addressing Conflict Is a Two-Way Street

Addressing issues that arise in your day-to-day life requires the development of both internal and external boundaries. ***The CORE model listed here involves both:***

C – External: Consider origins of THEIR Reality.
Internal: Consider origins of YOUR Reality.

O – External: opt Out –
Internal: Own the Outcome.

R – External: Remember your "why".

Internal: Refuse to blame others.

E – External: Establish healthy boundaries
Internal: Eliminate unhealthy filters.

As you become more familiar with your triggers, you will be in a much better position to properly handle each situation. The more you recognize these events playing out, the more disciplined you become in changing your reaction to a response, but only if you choose to put forth the effort in changing the way you see it.

Again, journaling is an excellent tool for identifying your triggers in each situation. It offers an opportunity to step back and assess the situation to determine how it came up and how to best resolve it, based on the parties involved. Once you take the time to journal a given situation, you are then able to address it in a healthy productive way.

Many of the thoughts you have were planted in your mind a long time ago. How you meditate on those thoughts will determine your beliefs about yourself, other people, and the world around you.

My Journal Entry:

I realize that my sister made a choice. We all make choices; some good, some not so good. When we respond based on our emotions, we make bad decisions. It's so important that we take the time to marinate on a particular situation by waiting until our emotions have a chance to calm down. When these emotions reach a level of calm, we can then begin to incorporate our minds to make sense of it all. Journaling provides a healthy outlet to assist in escalating this process.

SUMMARY

- If you don't stop long enough to discern each pile of dirt (the trauma from your past), you fail to understand how these experiences are influencing your current reality.

- Quite often, it's how we process our experiences that prevent us from living the life we imagined.

- Our triggers are our pre-conditioned beliefs about ourselves based on the painful experiences we have had in our past that surface when we feel victimized in one way or another.

  What triggers have you identified through reading this chapter?

  ____

  ____

  ____

  ____

  ____

  ____

  ____

  ____

- It's easier to place blame on our past than it is to claim victory over our future.

- There were times when we weren't allowed to defend ourselves. As adults, we now have an opportunity to defend ourselves but in a way that doesn't jeopardize our emotions, our livelihood or even our peace of mind.

  If fear were not an issue, how do you see yourself validating who you are in a way that does not jeopardize your emotions, your livelihood, or your peace of mind? ________________

  ____

  ____

  ____

  ____

  ____

  ____

- Once you take the time to journal a given situation, you are then able to address it in a healthy productive way.

  Journal how this validation for who you are can preserve your emotions, your livelihood, and your peach of mind.

  ____

  ____

  ____

  ____

  ____

  ____

  ____

  ____

  ____

  ____

- Using the C.O.R.E. model will help you to identify triggers so you can eliminate unhealthy filters and respond in a healthy manner.

Use the C.O.R.E. model to reflect on an experience that took a particular direction based on your trigger. How would this experience have been different? ____________________

____

____

____

____

____

____

C – Consider origins of YOUR Reality. ____________________

____

____

O – Own the Outcome. ____________________

____

____

R – Refuse to blame others. ____________________

____

____

E – Eliminate unhealthy filters. ____________________

____

____

- Many of the thoughts you have were planted in your mind a long time ago. How you meditate on those thoughts will determine your beliefs about yourself, other people, and the world around you.

Let us look at contrasting views: What do you see when you meditate on God's vision vs. meditating on the enemy's [worldly carnal] vision?

- *About Yourself?* ________________________________

____

____

____

____

____

____

- *About People?* ________________________________

____

____

____

____

____

- *About the world?* ______________________________

____

____

____

____

____

MAMA

CHAPTER 9

YOUR TOMORROW WAR

> Let's say God, in His infinite wisdom, chose the childhood for me. What then does He expect from me? How does He want me to live a life when I never felt loved or valued? I don't feel loved or valued by God because if He loved me, He wouldn't have cursed me with such a horrible sad childhood.
>
> Journal Entry, My Twin

My husband and I recently watched the movie The Tomorrow War with Chris Pratt. At first, I didn't think I would be able to watch it because of the aliens and how they were eating the people who were assigned to be soldiers to take back humanity from an alien takeover. This movie genre isn't exactly my cup of tea. Civilians with no previous military experience were pulled from all walks of life and sent into the future to fight a war against aliens who took over the world. While this movie may be considered fictional, given the element of time travel, let's consider the possibility.

How would our lives be different if we were able to travel into the future and see the damage caused by how we live right now? The most profound lesson gleaned from this movie, for me, was how the main character, Chris Pratt, was able to change the future. He was able to go back to a period of time when the aliens had not yet become a threat and destroy them before they even made it to that time.

What if we could do that for ourselves? What if the core of our human failures could be identified and altered before they wreaked havoc in our lives and the lives of those we love? We can. But only if we are willing to step back and consider how our own painful pasts can negatively contribute to the pain felt in the lives of those whom God has entrusted us with in the future.

How can the pain from our past affect the lives of our children and those we love in the future? No, we can't physically travel into the future, but we can anticipate. We can also identify patterns within our own family of origin that could negatively affect how the future turns out for those we love, either born or yet to be born.

What if we could eliminate the pain and confusion experienced by our offspring in the future? What if we could eliminate some of our own future pain? In this fictional movie, the main character was able to save his daughter from death in the future. Seeing how the future unfolded for his daughter and feeling the agonizing pain of her death gave him the courage to face his reality and find a way to change it. As a result, his daughter's life was altered. This precious child was given an opportunity to live free from a burden that was out of her control, a burden that was in the making long before she was even born.

You may never understand how your painful experiences from childhood have influenced your current reality. My hope is that you will take the time to consider how your painful experiences will impact the lives of your children. Whether you have children or plan to have them in the future, their emotional stability is in your hands. If you don't do the work for you, do it for them.

COLLATERAL DAMAGE

A question my therapist wants me to ask my inner child: What would your childhood be like if you had parents that loved and adored you?

If they were not drug abusers or alcoholics and valued education and were not lazy and both had intimate relationships with God through Jesus Christ, I would be a young child who is developing self-esteem, is intelligent and quick to learn. I would have a bedtime and be lucky enough to have her mother or father read to her a bedtime story before tucking me in and kissing me goodnight. And always ending by saying, "I love you, sweetheart."

Journal Entry, My Twin

Whenever a war is waged, there will be casualties. Collateral damage means any damage incidental to an activity (www.dictionary.com). When we fail to understand how we have carried these painful experiences into our adulthood, we create collateral damage that impacts the lives of everyone we love.

When a child tells you they have been abused in any way, believe them.

My mother experienced trauma at a young age through sexual abuse by both her father and her stepfather. When she tried to tell her mother, it was dismissed as a lie. This began the downward spiral of behavior that has continued throughout my mother's life.

My mother grew up in an era where familial sexual abuse was not "talked about". In his book, Woman, Thou Art Loosed,[11] which later became an American drama film, T.D. Jakes tells the history of a woman's struggle to come to terms with her legacy of abuse, addiction and poverty. When I read his book and watched this film, I couldn't help but see my mother through the eyes of this woman. While it gave me a clearer understanding of what she had gone through, it didn't change the pain of my own experiences as a result of her own.

My mother never understood how her past traumatic experiences impacted her three daughters. She never understood why she didn't have meaningful relationships with anyone. She held on to the role of victim and wore it like a badge of honor. In my upcoming book, The Ties that Keep Us Bound, I provide a vivid explanation of a dysfunctional model of behavior referred to as "the Drama Triangle". This model was created by Dr. Stephen Karpman[12] in 1967 and brings light to this model of behavior and how it is used to keep us in bondage to our past traumatic experiences. I began my research into this model of behavior to learn more about my own behavior and that of my family members. Once I understood this model, it became much easier to set clear, healthy boundaries.

Remember I told you about the dirty mop
water spreading all over the kitchen floor?
This is how the damage continues.

I ran away from home at nineteen years old because of my mother's physical and emotional abuse. This is when the residual effects of my childhood trauma began to rear their ugly heads. I was headed down a slippery slope that eventually led to my emotional healing.

I ran away to live with my boyfriend at the time. He and I met where I attended junior college at the suggestion of my twin sister who attended there. My sister also worked at the college bookstore and secured a position for me there, as well. One day, an extremely handsome young man walked into the bookstore where I was working between classes. I immediately fell in love. Little did I know that he had experienced childhood trauma himself but on a totally different level.

The falling in love was mutual. He had his own place and became my ticket out of the hellhole I called home. When I ran away, I moved in with him. This created a dramatic and volatile response from my mother, as one might imagine. One day, two years later, my mother visited our home and an argument ensued between her and my boyfriend. This altercation eventually led to my mother going after her gun that was in her purse in another room. My sister pleaded for my boyfriend to leave the house (our house) and he proceeded to exit out the front door. Despite my sister's pleading for my mother to stop, my mother followed him outside and began shooting at him in broad daylight.

I ran behind her as she rushed out of the house with gun in hand. I pleaded with her to stop. I stood next to her as she fired three shots. It was so surreal. I couldn't believe this was happening. By this time, my boyfriend had turned into an alley. When he heard a shot whiz past his ear, he began to run. It was at that point that I decided I couldn't continue a relationship with someone who was this evil and vindictive, no matter who it was. I ordered my mother to leave.

My boyfriend telephoned his mother, who instructed him to move to another state and take up residence with his grandparents for safety. I decided to go with him.

My boyfriend had career obligations and had to leave town ahead of me. I gave notice to my job and my landlord and began the moving process. The day after the shooting incident, my mother and I had a phone conversation in which I informed her that I was leaving. She proceeded to give me a choice. If I went with him she would disown me. "It's either him or me," she said. I chose him.

My mother had given me furniture and appliances to use in my apartment. After our altercation, she informed me that she was coming to get her things out of my apartment. I left a key in the mailbox so she could get her things while I was at work. I didn't want to see her.

The next day, when I came home from work, she had picked up all her items, including a stove and refrigerator. It really didn't dawn on me at the time, but she had disconnected a gas stove. I did not have the gas cut off. It was cold outside, and with no furniture, I slept by the gas heater to stay warm throughout the night.

MY TWIN SISTER SAVED MY LIFE

The next morning, my sister called me at work to find out if I was okay after having everything taken out of my home. I informed her of what our mother had taken and that I smelled gas. She called the gas company and met them at my apartment, since I had to work. They turned off the gas. They informed her that if the front door had been opened one more time, the place would have exploded.

Over the years, I would be reminded of how my mother's own childhood trauma dictated her actions toward me and my sisters. Because she never recognized the residual effects of her own trauma, she passed her unresolved pain and anger onto us. Just as the spilled bucket of water doesn't stop flowing, her unresolved issues spilled into every relationship she had.

If we aren't willing to come face to face with our own trauma and how it is impacting our lives as adults, we create our own internal and external chaos. This chaos then spews throughout all our relationships. This is how the vicious cycle of abuse continues.

MY WAKEUP CALL

When my son was 11 years old, I received an unexpected visit from a caseworker with a child protective services agency in that city. This caseworker sat in our family room and informed me that she had received a call from his school. My son had visited the nurse's office at school that morning. He was complaining of pain in his buttocks area as a result of a paddle beating by his stepfather, my husband at the time. She proceeded to show me pictures of the welts that were left behind on my son's buttocks because of the paddle my husband used on him. With my son in the room, she spoke to me sternly and stated that if I or my husband were to lay another hand on my son again, I would be taken into custody and my son would be taken away from me.

I was emotionally paralyzed. Fear took over my entire body and created a stronghold that can only be compared to a snake tightening around my torso. I gasped for air to breathe. I couldn't believe what was happening to me. This caseworker's words immediately triggered a stinging memory of my mother yelling and threatening me as a child. I felt humiliated, angry, sorrowful, and guilty.

As a part of the ongoing investigation of child abuse, I was mandated to attend six weeks of parenting classes. This experience proved to be a valuable turning point in my life. It was at this point that I realized how I was creating collateral damage in the lives of my children. I was repeating the same horrible conditions that I had experienced as a child. Even though I had vowed that I would NEVER treat my children the way my mother had treated me, I was continuing the same pattern of child abuse. I was duplicating the trauma I experienced into the lives of my children.

Sometimes, without even realizing it, we can create an environment for our children that imitates our own childhood dysfunction, a foundation for their own dysfunction. The only difference between my childhood and my children's childhood is that I allowed someone else to inflict the pain on them. I was too much of a coward to do it myself, so I looked for someone else to rescue me by inflicting that pain on my children for me.

It wasn't until I was mandated to complete this six-week parenting program that I began to see how I was duplicating my own childhood experiences. For the first time, I realized that I did not have a normal, healthy childhood. I completed this course realizing that I didn't have to raise my children the way I was raised. These mandatory classes were a welcome wakeup call and a turning point for me. While the child abuse case against me was declared "unfounded", I decided to leave my husband and begin a new life with my children in another state.

Even after completing these court ordered parenting classes, I continued to conduct my life in a way that was detrimentally harmful to my children's well-being. The foundation for childhood trauma in the lives of my own children had been laid.

I allowed the enemy to run rampant, thereby ruining the chance I had to make amends for the damage I had already done. Both of my children abandoned me at some point as a result of my abusing and abandoning them.

But when we know better, we do better, right?

SUMMARY

- What if we could eliminate the pain and confusion experienced by our offspring in the future?

  How would you feel about that? ______________________

  ____

  ____

  ____

  ____

  ____

  ____

  ____

  ____

- What if we could eliminate some of our own future pain?

  What would your life look like if you could? ____________

  ____

  ____

  ____

  ____

  ____

  ____

  ____

  ____

- You may never understand how your painful experiences from childhood have influenced your current reality. My hope is that you will take the time to consider how your painful experiences will impact the lives of your children.

- Sometimes, without even realizing it, we can create an environment for our children that imitates our own childhood dysfunction, a foundation for their own dysfunction.

  What generational patterns of dysfunction do you have the power to disrupt; for yourself and for your offspring? ____

  ____

  ____

  ____

  ____

- If we aren't willing to come face to face with our own trauma and how it is impacting our lives as adults, we create our own internal and external chaos. This chaos then spews throughout all our relationships. This is how the vicious cycle of abuse continues.

  What are you willing to do to disrupt the cycle of abuse? __

  ____

  ____

  ____

  ____

CHAPTER 10

CREATING HEALTHIER OUTCOMES

If Only I Knew Then What I Know Now...Then What?

Isn't that an interesting statement to reflect upon? It's one of those statements that takes us back through all the perceived mistakes we have made and gives us permission to dream of what might have been, IF ONLY.

IF ONLY I had finished school.

IF ONLY I had married my high school sweetheart.

IF ONLY I hadn't married my high school sweetheart.

IF ONLY I had followed my dream of _________ (you fill in the blank).

The problem with ***IF ONLY*** is that it negates the beautiful reality of the lessons we have learned along the way.

I was raised in a single parent home and raised two children as a single parent myself. Because of the lessons I learned through the perceived mistakes I made on my journey through life as a single parent, I made the decision to view each perceived mistake as a lesson learned rather than a mistake. I allowed God to show me how each one of these experiences has equipped me to carry out His unique plan for my life.

This life we live is one that affords us many opportunities to use the lessons we have learned to be a blessing to others, ***IF ONLY*** we will view them that way.

As a Boundaries Coach, I teach women how to set healthy boundaries in all areas of their lives, raising children alone, managing their time, their finances, and yes, even their relationships. My motto is,

"My job is not to wallow in your misery with you but to escort you out of it!"

Why? Because wallowing doesn't get us or our children anywhere but entrenched deeper in the muck of life's challenges. It's not until we understand where we are and how we got here that we find the courage to move toward living the victorious life that God has promised us. When we are ready to step out of our past and walk toward that victorious life, we position ourselves to positively alter not only our own lives but the lives of the people we touch. More importantly, we have the marvelous opportunity to navigate the course of our children's lives for generations to come.

Now that I am a grandparent, I can see the patterns of my own dysfunctional actions beginning to get passed on to my grandchildren. It is MY responsibility to break the cycle of dysfunction by identifying it, owning it, and taking the steps necessary, those which I CAN control, to ensure that my grandchildren do not repeat this cycle of dysfunction by carrying it into their adulthood and onto their children.

IF you knew then what you know now, would you be able to impact people's lives in a positive way as much as you can right now? Maybe not. You would not have made the choices that taught you the lessons you have learned.

The decisions you made and the lessons learned from them provide encouragement to others. Your perspective of your decisions, in hindsight, will help others to know they are not alone and that they can create good outcomes based on their own choices, as well.

If you only knew then what you know now AND you made different choices as a result, just imagine the beautiful experiences you would have missed out on along the way. You are right where you need to be in life. Embrace your journey and decide to share your amazing outcomes with others.

Excerpt from my Journal Entry:

The residual effects of our painful past can be devastating. They ARE devastating. We have no idea how our trauma will affect us or the people around us. But what's more important is that we don't pass on the remnants of that trauma onto innocent bystanders: our children, our spouses, all the people who love and care for us. We must make sure they are not abused, neglected, or manipulated due to our own toxic behavior.

The Battle through Four Generations of Women

> And I will put enmity between you and the woman, and between your offspring and her Offspring; He will bruise and tread your head underfoot, and you will lie in wait and bruise His heel. (Genesis 3:15)

Enmity (def.): A feeling or condition of hostility; hatred, ill will, animosity, antagonism

Several years ago, I read "The Bait of Satan" [13] a book written by John Bevere. In this book, the author exposes one of Satan's most deceptive schemes used to pull us out of the will of God. John refers to this scheme as the spirit of offense.

In his book "Outwitting the Devil"[14], Napoleon Hill delves even deeper into how the enemy uses the spirit of offense to divert our attention from God's will and under the enemy's power.

Reading these two books prompted me to create a family timeline. There's something about getting things out on paper, which is why I am so adamant about using journal writing as a tool for personal growth. In this case, I used a board, an easel and a box of dry-erase markers. I am a kinesthetic learner, so I learn better through application.

I began my family timeline with the year my grandmother was born. I proceeded to add the year my mother was born, then the year I was born. Lastly, I added the year my daughter was born. I created a timeline that included four generations of women. As I stepped back to view the timeline I had created, I realized that right in front of me, staring me in the face, was evidence of Satan's diabolical scheme to destroy my family and our legacy.

He had infiltrated the spirit of offense into our relationships.

I began to see a clear pattern. My strained relationship with my mother, my mother's strained relationship with her mother, and the strained relationship I created with my daughter. I recalled how any communication with my mother conjured up feelings of hurt, anger and resentment, no matter how hard I tried not to feel those emotions. At that moment, I found myself spiraling back down to the pit of my past and stationing myself there emotionally, feeling as though my hands have been handcuffed behind my back, unable to break free.

As Satan's work became clear, I cried out to God for answers. I didn't want my relationships with my mother and my daughter to be what they were. I wanted healthy, loving relationships with them, but I didn't know how to make that happen.

God then reminded me of the volatile relationship between my mother and my grandmother. When I step back to view the bigger picture, I can see that the enemy had been successful (thus far) in planting seeds of destruction throughout these four generations of women.

The first thought that came to me was the realization that the enemy had waged war, spiritual warfare against my family!

The first question that came to mind was "What had he prevented from happening as a result of his viscous attacks against the women in my family?" What greater works could my grandmother and mother have done had the enemy not interfered? What work could my daughter and I have done had it not been for Satan? What was he preventing us from doing?

Reading these two books, journaling and prayer gave me the information and the courage I needed to interrupt Satan's plan of destruction for my family. I knew I couldn't do it alone. I needed God to guide me through this process.

Sometimes, we try to win a war, but we don't equip ourselves with the right weapons. Just as David had become skilled in using a slingshot, I became skilled at using the power of the Holy Spirit to guide me. God has equipped us to use the power of the Holy Spirit to win any battle that the enemy wages against us. We must know how to use our weapons against him.

> "I have created the blacksmith who fans the coals beneath the forge and makes the weapons of destruction. And I have created the armies that destroy. But in that coming day no weapon turned against you will succeed. You will silence every voice raised up to accuse you. These benefits are enjoyed by the servants of the Lord; their vindication will come from me.
>
> I, the Lord, have spoken!" (Isaiah 54:16,17)

Prepared for Battle

I have seen Satan snatch so many people away from their purpose. If he can get you to react rather than respond to those that have offended you or hurt you, he can get you so wrapped up in that drama that you take your eyes off what's important. So much of the hurt we experience is merely a smoke screen and diabolical tactic that he uses to ensure you don't go anywhere near the path where you are supposed to walk.

So many people go through life without even a clue as to why they are here or what they're supposed to be doing while they are here. Then, there are those that know their purpose and begin walking towards it. Before they realize it, the enemy throws obstacles in the way, all meant to either delay them or take them completely off course. Those obstacles often show up in the form of relationships. God's command is that we love one another (John 15:17). If Satan can keep us from loving one another, he can keep us away from honoring God.

We are in a battle, and your enemy is out to destroy you....at any cost, by whatever means necessary. His goal is to take you out. He knows that he has been defeated in the end, but in the meantime, he will do whatever he can to destroy anyone who threatens his reign on this earth. Even though we already know who wins the battle, we often forget that there will be casualties. We don't have to be one of them. If we understand what we are fighting, who we are fighting and how we have been equipped as soldiers in God's Army, we don't have to be afraid. We are not expected to fight this battle alone (Deuteronomy 28:7). We are not expected to fight this battle in the natural, but in the supernatural.

IMPORTANT NOTE: We are fighting on Satan's turf, not our own. We have been dropped on this earth in a foreign land, the world. We can't expect to win it based on what we see in the natural. The only way to win is by understanding the power that has been placed within us. When Jesus died on the cross for you (yes YOU!), He placed within you the power and the ability to wrestle against principalities, not flesh and blood (those that we assume we are supposed to fight on this earth). When we attempt to win through our own might, we are destined to lose. Satan expects us to raise our white flag, tuck in our tails and run. Every time you subject yourself to the torment, ridicule and ill-treatment inflicted on you by others [through the dysfuntional model of behavior that Stephen Karpman refers to as the Drama Triangle], you take yourself further and further away from where you are supposed to be.

If you don't know what a battle is or can't relate to one, get in the habit of watching movies that educate you on the many battles people have faced and won, people who have come through insurmountable trials and overcome to the point of victory. These movies can range anywhere from the Disney movie, The Lion King to Enough with Jennifer Lopez. Begin to pay attention to the struggles and the victories that result from their fight and their decision to never give up, their determination to face every obstacle with courage.

As you watch these movies or any movie you choose, be on the lookout for:

1) the challenge(s) they faced

2) their opportunity to play victim and

3) how they made the decision to fight rather than to give up or give in, and

4) what they were fighting for. What was so important to them that they chose to fight?

As you identify the answers to these questions, consider your own storyline. While these stories may be fictional in nature, they paint a picture of the realities of life. They identify a dream, a struggle, and a victory. What is your dream, what is your struggle and which battle do you need to face to be victorious?

You may have had a dream to be a doctor, a lawyer, a writer, a dancer, a singer...I could name a few dreams. You fill in the blank for your own dream. Along the way, you may have had an obstacle dropped on your path that prompted you to take a detour because the obstacle seemed too big to step over. This obstacle grew into a wall, one that you could not see beyond.

At some point, you could no longer see that dream on the other side of that obstacle that had grown into a brick wall. You made the decision to settle for where you are.

You may have even begun to blame others for your decision to not fight through the obstacles. You may have made excuses so big that even you started to believe them.

You may have been persecuted so much by a victim that you fell into your comfortable role of giving up on your dream to rescue someone else from their own struggle.

Whichever choice you made, it took you further away from your dream, so you gave up. Who do you think is at the core of the scenarios that may have played out for you? Who stands to win the most when you give up on your dream? Most importantly, who stands to lose the most? When you fall victim to the manipulative tactics of the enemy, you step off the path toward your purpose.

So how do you get back on that path?

- You start by becoming clear about who you are and whose you are.
- You decide that you will NOT be a victim and that you will be victorious.
- You use your pain to be a blessing to others.
- You do not make excuses for where you are or where you came from.
- You put the world on notice that you are wonderfully made, and...
- You embrace the fact that you are a mighty woman of fearless courage!

Congratulations! You have officially entered the army of God as a warrior, a force to be reckoned with!

SUMMARY

- You have the marvelous opportunity to navigate the course of our children's lives for generations to come.

- God has equipped us to use the power of the Holy Spirit to win any battle that the enemy wages against us. We must know how to use our weapons against him.

What is your dream? ______________________________

____

____

____

____

What is your struggle? ____________________________

____

____

____

____

Which battle do you need to face to be victorious? _______

____

____

____

____

Chapter 11

CHOOSE YOUR BATTLES WISELY

> "For we do not wrestle against flesh and blood, but against principalities, against powers, against the rulers of the darkness of this age, against spiritual hosts of wickedness in the heavenly places." (Ephesians 6:12)

It's easy to think about the multitude of painful experiences we have had and blame our current discontent on our past failures. As you read this book, you are faced with re-living some of the most awful experiences you have ever had. I know you are, because that's exactly what happened to me while writing this book. I had to go through all my sister's recordings and journal entries. Each time I read her words or heard the helplessness in her voice through her recorded therapy sessions, it brought me to tears with a pain too deep to explain.

What's not easy is owning up to the responsibility, of ensuring that the dysfunctional pattern of behavior that was created for us does not get passed on to others. It's our responsibility to ensure that the cycle does not continue. How do we do that? By understanding our role in the battle and whom we are fighting against.

We are all in a battle, a battle so far-reaching and so massive that we don't even understand its full magnitude. In this battle, many are fighting blindfolded, not really understanding whom they are fighting against. Some realize the magnitude of the battle but are at a loss as to how to fight it.

Throughout my life, God has given me opportunities to help women whom the enemy has deceived into believing they are victims. The enemy has filled these women with so much fear that they become spiritually and emotionally paralyzed, unable to move forward. These women were placed on my path for a reason.

The Lord has given me authority to snatch souls out of Satan's grasp and to deliver them back into His arms. He has used me to show them what Satan is doing to them and how he is manipulating them and preventing them from fulfilling God's purpose for their lives.

> "You must warn each other every day, while it is still "today," so that none of you will be deceived by sin and hardened against God." (Hebrews 3:13)

God has given me a voice and a presence to expose Satan's lies so that people's lives are meaningful for the purposes God has for each of them. Satan has many lying in a deep sleep, unconsciously meandering through life like zombies, just accepting what life is handing them, because it's offering them nothing but mediocrity. You were created for so much more than that!

In his book The War of Art[125], Steven Pressfield writes about people dying and never accomplishing any of their dreams, let alone the purpose that God had for them. Why? Because they allowed the enemy to sabotage their acceptance of who they really were and the talents they really possessed. Very few people have the fortitude to fight the battle to pursue their purpose. They allow their limited, unchallenged knowledge to dictate where they will end up in life.

God has equipped me to fight. He has placed inside me everything I need to win this battle. Most importantly, He has given me the courage to help YOU win your battle, as well.

You must remain open to learning, open to realizing that there is so much more than what you see in front of you. Once you begin to look outside of yourself and your environment, you can seek out new roads, new opportunities for growth and discoveries that are far beyond anything you could have imagined. Let me be the vessel to help you uncover and release your authentic power. How do you do that? By:

1. Getting comfortable in your own skin
2. Assuming a new fighting position
3. Revealing the warrior within you
4. Developing the warrior within you

5 Activating the warrior within you

The Greatest Diversion

As you begin to understand the magnitude of your childhood experiences, I want you to place blame where it belongs. It's not in the people who caused you harm. It's in the strategies that the enemy has devised to keep you in bondage to your past, unable to move beyond it.

Life hands challenges to everyone. Not all challenges are attributed to Satan, only those that create residual damage because of our childhood experiences. As we enter adulthood, our painful pasts manifest in different ways, bringing challenges all their own. My challenges came in how I raised my children. Others have experienced challenges through obstacles set before them: Disease, poverty, drugs, incest, sexual abuse, mental or physical illness or even murder, just to name a few. Everyone is fighting their own demons.

One day, while reflecting on my own battles, I sat down and wrote a poem. I want to share it with you:

Where have you been? Where are you going?

How are you affected by the demons in your life?

You have them, I have them. Where do they begin?

I've identified my demons, can you identify yours?

If you don't, they will look for you.
They will consume you and devour you.
Don't let them.

Search for them. Find them.
Magnify them. Illuminate them, expose them.

Peer into the porthole of the demon house.
How many are out there, running around, frolicking in your life causing chaos and despair?

Your demons are like little children in a classroom when the teacher walks out of the room, jumping out of their seats and scattering throughout the room, getting into things and places where they don't belong. Come back into the room, teacher. Watch the little demons go back to their seats.

Come back to yourself. Face your demons head on.
See them for what they truly are.

What do they look like? Assess their size.
Are they bigger than you?

I once knew a demon, strong and tall.

He claimed victory over my soul.

He set up house in this body of mine,

an uninvited guest, wearing out his welcome.

This demon inhaled my energy and
wreaked havoc throughout my home.

I tried to keep clean my thoughts,
my dreams, and my intentions.

He scattered dust onto my every attempt at a clear
vision into my core to block my view.

This demon has found a resting place,
but he did not come empty handed.

He is armed with a magnifying glass in his hand.

While I am resting, He uses this magnifying glass to
awaken me to my vulnerability and despair.

My weaknesses are enlarged by
his magnified view of them,

forcing me to retreat into my room, surrendering
to his strategy, giving him complete run of my domain.

It's time to clean house.

It's time to muster the energy necessary to open the blinds and allow light to enter the windows.

It's time to expose the dust, the dirt, and the demons in your house.

God has allowed me to be the bridge from which His blessings flow. I am stretching out my hand so you can grab it. Don't be afraid to stick your hand out. Trust that I can get you to the other side, that place where God's comfort resides, that place of refuge, safe from the torments of the enemy and the snare of his entangled constraints that are preventing you from moving forward. Don't be one of those who would rather stay stuck right where they are. Too many people are biding time…for WHAT?

THE FIGHT OF YOUR LIFE

The decision to break the cycle of residual damage passed on to others is a courageous one. I commend you for your amazing courage. The beauty of this battle is that you are not fighting it alone. God is waiting to be called into the battle.

So, we can say with confidence, "The Lord is my helper, so I will have no fear. What can mere people do to me? (Hebrews 13:6)

Now that you know who's with you, stand firm. The steps you now take to break the cycle of dysfunction will prove to be the most important steps you will ever take.

SUMMARY

- It is our responsibility to ensure that the dysfunctional pattern of behaviors that were created for us do not get passed on to others.

- It's our responsibility to ensure that the cycle does not continue. How do we do that? By understanding our role in the battle and whom we are fighting against.

  *What is YOUR role?*____________________________________

- You must remain open to learning, open to realizing that there is so much more than what you see in front of you.

- Once you begin to look outside of yourself and your environment, you can seek out new roads, new opportunities for growth and discoveries that are far beyond anything you could have imagined. This is how you expand your boundaries.

  How do you see yourself expanding your boundaries? ____

  ____

  ____

  ____

  ____

  ____

  ____

- Life hands challenges to everyone. Not all challenges are attributed to Satan, only those that create residual damage as a result of our childhood experiences.

  What challenges are you facing that have nothing to do with your childhood experiences? ______________________

  ____

  ____

  ____

  ____

  ____

  ____

How do you know? ______________________________

____

____

____

____

____

____

What can you do about them? ____________________

____

____

____

____

____

____

- The steps you now take to break the cycle of dysfunction will prove to be the most important steps you will ever take.

  What is the first step you can take (big or small) to disrupt the cycle of dysfunction in your family? ____________

____

____

____

____

____

____

____

____

Chapter 12

The Process of Healing

> I may have been raised in a dysfunctional family home, but I'm not damaged because of it.
>
> Journal Entry, My Twin

Your past doesn't dictate your future,
only the platform from which you launch.
Pamela L. Byrd

After reading through all my twin sister's journals and listening to volumes of recorded therapy sessions between her and her therapist, I now possess a greater understanding of why she chose to end her life.

No matter how identical we were in our blood, we were fraternal in our approach to healing from our painful childhood experiences. We both sought answers that would help us to heal, but we were different in our belief of how we could overcome our painful pasts.

My sister chose to stay close to her abusers out of fear that they would hurt her even more, while I chose to distance myself from those who abused me out of a different kind of fear. Because of how she was treated as a child and how she allowed others to treat her as an adult, she didn't feel that she deserved much more than what others were willing to give her. She believed she was unworthy of love from anyone, even God. It's impossible to believe that anyone loves you if you don't love yourself.

I, on the other hand, never doubted that God loved me unconditionally. Somehow, I knew that He had an ultimate plan for my life. I felt that if God loved me, I could learn to love myself, no matter how others made me feel. So, I learned how to fight. I learned how to use the weapons that He provided to me. While I have contemplated suicide a few times, I never followed through on those thoughts. Whenever I felt like giving up, I would go through my pity party, cry, wail, journal and pray (In that order). When I woke up the next morning, I was energized and ready to take on whatever life threw my way. I was determined to not allow my painful past to dictate my future. I never wanted to give Satan that satisfaction. I knew that God had equipped me to do great things.

When you were born, you were given the power to do great things. Somehow, the enemy stepped in and snatched that power away from you, but you can get it back. You can reclaim it. I know you can, because I did. You must first decide that you are worthy of this power, no matter how much of it has been stripped of you. You must then be ready to heal from your childhood trauma.

As I close, I want to offer options that you can choose from as you begin your healing process. Each option you choose will move you closer to eliminating the residual effects of childhood trauma so you can then reclaim your authentic power.

Embrace your Mental Health

Your painful childhood experiences impact your mental health. When you accept this fact, you can then begin to take the steps necessary to heal. When you refuse to accept the reality of the way these experiences are playing a role in how your life is playing out, when you ignore the results or blame others, you are setting yourself up for a life full of disappointments.

Lean on Me or Someone

Finding the right person to support you in your process of healing is critical. Do you have a friend or a family member that you can be honest with, one who will listen and is not afraid to be honest with you? Do you have a friend who is willing to hold you accountable to staying true to your desire to heal? If not, do not feel bad. Not everyone is capable of being that person for you. So many people are going through their own issues, unaware of how to work through them.

I am always here! As you have learned throughout this book, I have fought my battle and have been blessed to help others who need the support, encouragement and the accountability partner required to get you through the healing process. Reach out to me for a complimentary session so we can begin your healing journey.

Consider Therapy

Many have allowed their cultural norms to dictate the level of help they seek from mental health professionals. These cultural norms have convinced them that seeking therapy makes them weak. This fallacy is exactly what keeps us stuck in the hell we find ourselves enduring. Making the decision to seek therapy is a smart one. I am proud to admit that I have sought therapy on many occasions throughout my life. Working with a qualified mental health professional has given me a perspective about my situation(s) that I would have never considered on my own.

When you decide to seek therapy, understand that finding the right therapist is just as critical as committing to the process. The bond you create between you and your therapist will have a major impact on your growth. My sister saw several therapists. Not all of them were a good fit. I have listed a number of things to consider when seeking the right therapist for your situation:

A. **Consult your provider directory**. If your employer provides insurance coverage for these services, consult your providers network. If you don't have access to this type of coverage, be sure to include the cost of your therapist in your budget. Too many people refuse to get the help they need because of the cost. When you regard therapy as an investment in your future mental well-being, you learn to make this financial investment a priority.

B. **Ask someone you trust.** A recommendation from a friend, a doctor or a colleague is a wonderful place to start. Keep in mind that the person who is recommending a therapist may have a different situation from yours, so proceed accordingly.

C. **Use a reliable online database.** As mental health becomes more of a mainstream topic, more databases have been created to assist in finding licensed therapists. Be sure to peruse these databases carefully to ensure that you are finding therapists who specialize in your area of focus.

D. Explore local resources. There are advocacy groups in your area that can help you to get the support you need, resources that you may have never realized existed before. Have you ever bought a car and begun to see other cars on the road just like yours, cars you may have never seen before? The same revelation happens when we begin to seek out anything. There is more there than we ever realized. It's not until we form a desire that these similarities begin to reveal themselves to us at the time when we need them most.

E. Ask questions. Understand that the therapist you choose must earn your trust. The American Psychological Association suggests a few questions for you to consider asking your therapist during your first session:

1. Are you a licensed psychologist in this state?
2. How many years have you been in practice?
3. How much experience do you have working with people who are dealing with [the issue you'd like to resolve]?
4. What do you consider to be your specialty or area of expertise?
5. What kinds of treatments have you found effective in resolving [the issue you'd like resolved]?

6. Which insurance do you accept?
7. Will I need to pay you directly and then seek reimbursement from my insurance company, or do you bill the insurance company?
8. Are you part of my insurance network?
9. Do you accept Medicare or Medicaid?

Having your prospective therapist answer these questions will help you in your decision-making process. If you do not feel comfortable with this person, it is perfectly okay to try someone else. This is YOUR future and well-being at stake.

F. Make sure you are ready. Your commitment to therapy will get difficult. The issues that surface may be frightening. This is when you must remember the reason you made this commitment, in the first place. Giving up will only place you right back into the spiraling cycle of pain that brought you to therapy.

Set a goal for what you would like to achieve. I remember writing down my goals for therapy and sharing them with my new therapist. By the end of our 6-week period of working together, I had accomplished the goals I set out to achieve. She and I were able to partner in a much more productive way once she understood what I wanted to achieve.

Seek To Understand

Going through my sister's tape recordings, I came across a conversation she recorded between her and me. In this conversation, I was trying to get her to understand how our mother's childhood trauma impacted the way she raised us. I wanted her to view our abuse from a distinct perspective, our mother's perspective. My goal was to get my sister to begin focusing on her life now and to stop blaming someone else for where she was in her life at that time. As I listened to this recorded conversation, I realized that she was not at a place where she could accept the information I was sharing with her.

Nevertheless, it is important that we consider other facets of our childhood experiences. Understanding the trauma our mother experienced gave me a better understanding of why she behaved the way she did toward us. While it does not excuse her behavior, it does give me a broader perspective.

Whatever trauma you experienced as a child, consider the other side. What was it about the situation, the person, the person's history that could have contributed to their behavior? This will help you to gain a much clearer perspective, one that may help you in your healing process.

Take Parenting Classes

Whether you have children, plan to have children, or love someone who has children, consider taking parenting classes. I was forced to take parenting classes because of my son's physical abuse allegations. As I indicated earlier, taking this course was one of the best things that ever happened to me. My sisters and I had no idea what it was like to grow up in a healthy home environment. What I learned through these classes helped me to be a better mother and ultimately an amazing grandmother. It shouldn't take a court system to mandate parenting classes. Take the initiative to attend these classes on your own. It will give you new insights into how to parent appropriately.

Distance Yourself

It may be necessary to distance yourself from the co-dependent behavior of others to heal and grow stronger. Continuing to stay close to a person or situation that triggers painful emotions is not healthy for your healing process. It is up to you how and when to distance yourself. It is also your choice how you communicate your decision to others. How long you choose to distance yourself will depend on the time you need to gain the knowledge and strength you need to improve your level of emotional health.

Here's a fact you may not realize: Not everyone wants you to heal. There are those within your circle who would rather you stay where you are, just so they can have someone to relate to on their level of victimhood. Determine who these people are and distance yourself from them as much AND as soon as possible.

Take Care of YOU

Why do flight attendants instruct you to place the oxygen mask on your face first in the case of an emergency? You cannot be of service, support or help to anyone else, unless YOU are okay. To be at your best, you must take care of you. Incorporate a few forms of self-care into your daily or weekly routine. Make these things and times a priority in your life, not just something you do when you find the time. Trust me, if you do not make it a priority, you will NEVER find the time. You are important enough to indulge in self-care. My life-balance wheel includes time for self-care. This way, I am sure to take the time I need because it has been set aside and accounted for.

Journal Your Journey

As a journaling practitioner for the past 40 years, I cannot express enough the importance of journaling. Your ability to get your thoughts out of your head and down on paper is a tool that the enemy does not want you to use. Rereading and reflecting on your written words help you to identify patterns of behavior that the enemy does not want you to see. If he can prevent you from seeing the patterns that are detrimental to your growth, he can keep you stuck right where you are. My YouTube channel as well as my private FB Group the Journaling Suite offer insights and instructions on different journaling styles and how to use them for personal, spiritual, and emotional growth. The practice of journaling has given me the revelations I needed to re-claim my authentic power and to combat the enemy's lies.

You will want to document this journey you find yourself on right now. Who knows, one day, your words might be just what someone else needs to regain their own authentic power.

Help Someone Else

There are so many people around you who can benefit from your help. We can get so caught up in our own misery that we do not take the time to help anyone else. The beauty in helping others offers many benefits. It helps us to be a blessing to others, and it allows us to realize how truly blessed we are.

Helping someone else doesn't have to cost you anything, but the rewards are immeasurable. Take some time to call someone who you have been thinking about. If you can't call them, text them. If someone needs a ride, volunteer to take them. There are so many small things you can do to help someone. Helping others goes a long way in taking our mind off our own misery and helping someone else to gain a better perspective of their own.

Seek God.

> "Seek the Kingdom of God above all else, and live righteously, and he will give you everything you need." (Matthew 6:33 NLT)

I cannot imagine getting to where I am right now, based on where I came from, had it not been for my relationship with God. This bible verse tells you how God works. It also tells you how to benefit from His works, yep, that middle part, "and live righteously." If we don't take the time to know God – if we don't seek Him, we won't know what righteous living looks like. The world wants us to live according to its standards and Satan wants us to believe that these standards are valid. God wants us to live according to His standards. Seeking to build a relationship with God helps us to differentiate between the carnal (worldly view) and the spiritual (God's view). The only way we can truly understand the difference between the two is through seeking God. Only then are we poised and positioned to receive the blessings that God promises us in His Word.

Through my commitment to seeking God, I am getting stronger every day. I know that when the time comes for me to face my past, my family, He will give me the courage and the strength I need. I know that the Holy Spirit will season my emotions and responses in a way that gives glory to God, not the enemy. You see, the enemy wants me to be upset. He wants to rub my past in my face. What he needs to know is that my past doesn't prevent my wonderful future from happening. It only provides the backdrop from which I launch.

Find the Good

It is easier to focus on the bad experiences we had rather than how we came out of them. You have endured, survived, persevered, overcome and conquered. YOU are the bomb.com! How did you do it? Which qualities, gifts, talents and beliefs do you possess that have brought you to where you are today? Most importantly, how can you use these qualities, gifts, talents, and beliefs to take you to your next level? When we can find the good that came out of all that we endured, we can then begin to seek out avenues for becoming a blessing to others.

Let Go

There are times when we must choose to let go, to detach ourselves from the people who diminish our self-worth or from the situations that don't allow us to flourish the way we would like to. When we have attempted to distance ourselves, but the distance doesn't seem to be enough, it may be time to detach. I detach myself from certain people or situations to keep me strong...to protect me.

I grew up afraid of my mother. I grew up with a dis-taste for her. I attempted to work through it many times, even relocating her near me. I was doing it from the heart. I did it because I thought it was the right thing to do. I kept my eyes and ears open for signs that I might be spiraling down a path that I did not want to fall into. I continued to set healthy boundaries with her. Unfortunately, she was not willing to honor those boundaries, so my stress level increased.

The level of stress I experienced being around her began to affect my relationship with others, especially my husband. Just like that bucket of dirty mop water, my strained relationship with her began to spill over into my other important relationships. It was at this point when I realized that I had not achieved the level of healing I needed to have a loving relationship with her. Many people have asked about the difference between my sister and me because of our different outcomes. I can honestly say that one of the most significant differences is that I chose to detach from my mother while my sister chose to allow our mother to stay in her life.

I am not perfect. No one is perfect. I am no different from you. I am still working on letting go and letting God do the work. I know that healing takes time, but continuing to allow toxic behavior to jeopardize my healing process is not something I choose to do.

I have a very unhealthy relationship with my mother. I have chosen to detach from her because it's something I need for myself right now. I don't want to go back to a dysfunctional relationship because of a codependent upbringing.

My sister's death has prompted me to think about my childhood, but I won't allow the enemy to take me back there. I move forward.

For you to move forward, you must gather strength from God for the times when you must face your past. God will take your mess and turn it into your ministry but only If you ask Him.

MY SISTER IS NO LONGER WITH ME, BUT GOD IS.

> When Moses died, God said to Joshua, "Moses is gone, you are in charge now. Be strong and courageous for I am with you. I will not fail you or abandon you." (paraphrased), (See Joshua 1:1-9)

I write this book to honor my sister's life, her struggles, her selflessness, and her capacity to love unconditionally. Losing her has given me the courage I need to do what God has placed me on this earth to do. Loving her has given me the strength to honor her life in a way that she could not have possibly imagined.

Losing my sister has taken me out of a holding pattern. It has allowed me to see how important it is for me to share our experiences so that others can obtain emotional healing. God has given me the courage I need to be transparent and to share our story with you.

Our lives are at stake. The lives of our children are at stake. I would be doing an injustice to my sister if I did not use our story as a platform to help others to make sense of their own trauma and the residual effects of those traumatic experiences.

I believe God was with my sister throughout her life and even the day she gave up and took her last breath. I believe she is with Him now. I hear people say that their loved ones who have passed on are still with them. Personally, I don't believe that. I don't want my sister's spirit to be here. I want her spirit to be where she is, having God love on her like she has never been loved on before. I believe that she is so wrapped up in his love and continuously surrounded by the love of those whom she loved that passed on before her.

I don't want her to even think of me. I want her to know when she sees me again that I heard her cries and that when the time was right, I shared her story, and that I put aside my own fears to tell it. God has given me that courage.

I have not revealed the entire story, only the parts I have been prompted to share. It is my prayer that you will take from our story and do what is in your heart to break the cycle of trauma in your life for the sake of those here and those to come.

God Bless You, always.

CONTRACT FOR HEALING

I have provided options that you can choose from as you begin your healing process. The option(s) you choose will move you closer to eliminating the residual effects of childhood trauma so you can then reclaim your authentic power.

On the line(s) below, write down the options you are considering and what steps you will take to begin your healing journey. Be sure to include the date you plan to take each specific action.

Sign your commitment. Remove this page from the book and hang it somewhere where you can see it every day.

I commit to: ____

____

____

____

____

____

____

Signature: ____________________________ Date: __________

NOTES

Chapter One:

1. Karen Casey, "Let Go Now, Embracing Detachment" (ReadHowYouWant.com Ltd., May 2011).
2. Carolyn Myss, "Sacred Contracts, Awakening Your Divine Potential" (Harmony/Rodale, January, 2003)

Chapter Two:

3. Adverse Experiences and Trauma, (CEU Course www.YouTube.com: AllCeus Counseling & Education, January 13, 2021)
4. Lana Alibabic, "Three Types of Trauma", (www.edmchicago.com/what-it-trauma, January 3, 2022)

Chapter Four:

5. Jeff Olson, "The Slight Edge, Secrets to a Successful Life", (Momentum Media, 2005)

Chapter Five:

6. Jane Fonda, "Prime Time", (Random House, August 9, 2011)
7. Malcolm Gladwell, "tThe Unheard Story of David & Goliath", (www.ted.com, TED SALON, New York 2013)

Chapter Seven:

8. Hillary I. Lebow, "16 Codependent Traits That Go Beyond Being a People Pleaser", (www.psychcentral.com, July 22, 2021)

9. Pia Mellody, "Facing Codependence, What it is, Where it Comes From, and How it Sabotages our Lives," (Harper & Row, April 29, 2003)

Chapter Eight:

10. Rick Warren, "The Purpose Driven Life, What on Earth am I Here For?", (Zondervan, October 8, 2002)

Chapter Nine:

11. T.D. Jakes, "Woman Thou Art Loosed, Healing the Wounds of the Past", (Bethany House, 1996)
12. Stephen Karpman, "A Game Free Life, The Definitive book on the Drama Triangle", (Drama Triangle Publications, 2014)

Chapter Ten:

13. John Bevere, "The Bait of Satan, Living Free from the Deadly Trap of Offense", (Charisma House, January 1, 2012)
14. Napoleon Hill, "Outwitting the Devil, The Secret to Freedom and Success", (Sterling Publishing, 2011)

Chapter Eleven:

15. Steven Pressfield, "The War of Art", (Black Irish Entertainment, LLC, April 04, 2019)

Coming Soon

The Ties That Keep Us Bound

Breaking Free from Toxic Behaviors & Into Your Circle of Peace

This book focuses on women and the challenges they face in seeking and walking in their purpose. Pamela provides a thorough description of the "Drama Triangle" and how the three positions within this model of dysfunctional behavior may prevent us from walking in our purpose.

You will learn how to identify key characteristics exhibited in each position and the different roles they play with the people in our lives and how to set the boundaries needed to eliminate the drama that prevents us from walking in our God-given purpose.

ABOUT THE AUTHOR

Pamela Byrd is a Boundaries Coach and Journaling Practitioner. She teaches women how to identify the areas in their lives where healthy boundaries are needed to live life more abundantly.

She has been journaling since age 11 and teaches women how to use journal writing as a tool for building the confidence and courage needed to reclaim their authentic power. She believes that it's only through your healing from traumatic experiences that you can set healthy boundaries.

Pamela is married and together she and her husband Tyrone have a blended family of 7 children and 15 grandchildren. She enjoys reading, writing, crochet, watching 4K nature videos, and spending quality time with her family, not necessarily in that order.

"I Had a Twin" is her first book. She will launch her next book, "The Ties that Keep Us Bound" within the next year.

Pamela would love to hear how this book has impacted you. Send your comments to Pamela@theanswerswithinme.com

letstalkboundaries　Youtube.com/c/PamelaByrd

www.TheAnswersWithinMe.com　letstalkboundaries

Made in the USA
Columbia, SC
20 April 2022